Praise for {Why} N

For years I've wished I could live next door to September McCarthy. She is the mother we all want to grow up to be, and this book is the next best thing to sitting at her kitchen table. For every mom who's wanted a mentor, a big mama sister, and a practical guide all rolled into one, get ready to be fed. Here comes the mother lode of guilt-free advice from the mother to moms everywhere.

Lisa-Jo Baker, bestselling author of *Never Unfriended* and *Surprised by Motherhood*

The labor of motherhood never ends and sometimes it's hard to remember how to breathe. These pages are like a breathing coach. And each page is a delivery—into more and more of the grace and heart of your Father. Motherhood matters—because what matters like sculpting souls with your Father?

Ann Voskamp, mama to 7, *New York Times* bestselling author of *The Broken Way* and *One Thousand Gifts*

September's beautiful words about the journey of motherhood will touch deep places in your heart, provide sympathy for the struggles you have felt, and offer joy and vision to the role that is so profoundly important. You will find in her own personal stories a friend who walks the journey of motherhood by your side.

Sally Clarkson, author of *The Lifegiving Home* and *Different*

September McCarthy has the heart of a mama, the words of an encourager, and the wisdom of a friend who truly understands the journey. I believe all women are mothers in some way, and no matter which season of motherhood you're in, *Why Motherhood Matters* is an affirmation and celebration of one of the most beautiful, powerful roles we have as women.

Holley Gerth, bestselling author of *Coffee for Your Heart* and *You're Already Amazing*

It's rare to read a book on mothering that causes tears to stream down your face and fills you with gratitude and a profound reverence for the gift and calling of mother-hood. September has known real loss, real love, and ultimately real and authentic life deep in the trenches of raising ten children. September is my mom-hero! Her book is chock-full of practical wisdom, heart-wrenching stories, deep love for God and her family, and practical applications every mother will value. Let September's words advise, fill, encourage, and help you as you navigate motherhood with purpose and grace.

Kate Battistelli, author of *Growing Great Kids*, mother of Grammy Award winning artist Francesca Battistelli

In recent years, there has been a resurgence among Christians about the subject of "calling"—specifically, the integration of faith and work. Strikingly absent from these books, conferences, and conversations is the unique calling and vocation of motherhood. Enter September McCarthy, who is both writer and practitioner on this essential, image-of-God-bearing art. September does a magnificent job helping us reclaim motherhood as no ordinary calling, but a supreme one. Combining practical wisdom and the application of God's grace, she has provided women and men alike with a must-read.

Scott Sauls, senior pastor of Christ Presbyterian Church in Nashville, author of *Befriend*

I wish I'd had this book my first ten years of parenting. It's a game changer! This book points to gospel-based parenting with practical and encouraging steps for even seasoned moms to take.

Kristen Welch, author of *Raising Grateful Kids in an Entitled World*

As moms, we need other women—to sit with us, encourage us, and remind us that what we do today matters because it shapes the world tomorrow. Even before I met September, I was touched by her tender, mothering heart when she reached out and spoke words that gave life. Now as I call her my friend, I can say that I wholly trust her hard-fought wisdom and experience. She is a treasure among women. and if you don't believe me, then know that the very children she has mothered in her home rise up and call her blessed as well. That's a hearty endorsement!

Logan Wolfram, speaker, author of *Curious Faith*

Am I doing this right? Is any of this going to matter? As a mom of ten children I ask these questions often. *Why Motherhood Matters* is a gift to every mom. A gift that says "Remember your purpose. You don't have to do this alone. Follow your motherheart, which God's birthed inside you." September packs this book with help, inspiration, and God's truth to carry mothers through everyday struggles and hard seasons. I highly recommend it!

Tricia Goyer, *USA Today* bestselling author of *Walk it Out*

This is more than a book about motherhood. It's a poured-out offering from a soul who's known the deep sorrow of loss and surrendered dreams. But from the grave of those dreams a sanctifying journey begins that culminates in a life of love and sacrifice and beauty—a life that sees motherhood as the gift it is, not only to receive but to give again and again. No matter where you are in your own journey of spiritual nurturing, the words on these pages are for you.

Denise Hughes, author of the Word Writers® series and *Deeper Waters*

September meets us in the questions and struggles we wrestle through as moms, and with the comfort of a friend and the practical wisdom of a mentor, leads us to see the purposes of God in our calling. Find both encouragement and counsel in this book...a true companion to your motherhood journey.

Ruth Chou Simons, author of *GraceLaced*

{WHY}
MOTHERHOOD
MATTERS

September McCarthy

HARVEST HOUSE PUBLISHERS
EUGENE, OREGON

Cover by Connie Gabbert Design + Illustration

Cover Image © Floral Deco / Shutterstock

Interior design by Janelle Coury

September McCarthy is published in association with William K. Jensen Literary Agency, 119 Bampton Court, Eugene, Oregon 97404.

WHY MOTHERHOOD MATTERS

Copyright © 2017 September Anne McCarthy
Published by Harvest House Publishers
Eugene, Oregon 97402
www.harvesthousepublishers.com

ISBN 978-0-7369-7006-8 (pbk.)
ISBN 978-0-7369-7007-5 (eBook)

Library of Congress Cataloging-in-Publication Data
Names: McCarthy, September, author.
Title: Why motherhood matters / September McCarthy.
Description: Eugene, Oregon : Harvest House Publishers, 2017. | Includes
   bibliographical references.
Identifiers: LCCN 2017011327 (print) | LCCN 2017027020 (ebook) | ISBN
   9780736970075 (ebook) | ISBN 9780736970068 (pbk.)
Subjects: LCSH: Motherhood—Religious aspects—Christianity. |
   Mothers—Religious life. | Parenting—Religious aspects—Christianity. |
   Child rearing—Religious aspects—Christianity.
Classification: LCC BV4529.18 (ebook) | LCC BV4529.18 .M365 2017 (print) |
   DDC 248.8/431—dc23
LC record available at https://lccn.loc.gov/2017011327

Contents

Part III {Why} You Will Lead Them in the Way They Should Go

Part IV {Why} Giving Your Children a Reason to Change Makes All the Difference

For every woman...
born with a mother's heart
to be birthed in God's will and God's time.

For my daughters and my sons' wives,
my granddaughters, and the next generation,
this book is for your future.
It is my earnest prayer and abundant hope you will
embrace motherhood and everything it will offer you.

To my builder. My rock and protector of my heart.
We did this together.

{WHY}
Every Woman
Has a Mother's Heart

I feel as if I know you.

I have talked to you in the line at the grocery store. I have watched you sit alone at the park while your children play, and I have heard your story on the soccer sidelines. You and me? We have passed in the grocery line, with babies tied to our hips and teenagers asking for the keys to drive home. Your heart was knit with mine as we rocked on my front porch and cried tears of solidarity. You might be the woman I noticed mentoring teens at the local youth event, or the grandmother treating her grandson to lunch and listening ever so patiently. I see you. I hear you and I get it. Motherhood, in every season, is hard—and I do not believe we should do this alone.

We are coming together here, wondering the very same thing. *Will any of this ever make a difference?* There are days I have questioned if this thing called motherhood really matters. *Am I doing this right?* There must be more to the everyday, more behind the feelings of insecurity, and more answers than questions.

The repetitive work of everyday investment seems more like servanthood than an accumulation of earnings or rewards for the commitment and diligence. The truth is that most anything worth investing in will require us to become low in order to rise up. And when I rise up in my efforts in motherhood, I want them to mean something. To matter. To not just be an offering, but a sacrifice. That is what we do with gifts. We use them. We treasure them. And we give them over to God.

Motherhood is a gift that flows both ways. We do the giving and might wait years to feel we are receiving. We could possibly be missing the gift in the giving; and while we wait for the feeling of return on our investment, we are losing the moments that matter. I have watched woman after woman carry a beautiful dream in her heart, and then become embittered when the dream let her down and didn't meet her greatest expectations. On the outside, it may have looked as if she had everything any woman could want, but on the inside, the crushing reality that her dreams would never be realized turned her vision into one big disappointment.

I have heard it all.

This is what it all boils down to: Motherhood may disappoint you if you are unsure of your purpose.

I have lived inside those pockets of disappointment, discontentment. I have watched dreams pass me by. I have walked through womanhood wondering when I would feel that fulfillment everyone talks about.

Even after I became a mother, I wondered why motherhood mattered so much. Perhaps this is you and you get this. You feel the rawness that tugs at every woman's heart when she doesn't know the why.

Women with children talk about the early days of motherhood and their lack of purpose in the moments of sleep deprivation and diaper changes.

Women who are single or childless grieve the loss of their close-to-heart dreams.

Women with an untimed pregnancy spend years grieving the loss of time, plans, and desires to dream bigger.

And the women watching all of us, as we stir the pot of disappointment together, ask themselves, "Why would I ever begin to birth a dream or be brave enough to think that motherhood mattered?"

Why? This is the universal question that leads us to search and discover the gift God gave to every woman: a mother's heart. It's what we do with it that matters.

Why?

This is the universal question that leads us to search and discover the gift God gave to every woman: *a mother's heart.*

God's Why Holds Purpose

My marriage's beginnings were marked with repeated pregnancy loss, which left me wondering all the more why motherhood mattered. The emptiness of my womb sent me searching in deep places to find the answers in my own story and the bigger picture ahead.

How could I invest so much love and care and not see the fruit? Would there ever be a day when I knew it was all going to be okay? Why was I doing all of this anyway?

And then God gave me the *why*.

With my story, there is surrender in loss. It is a story woven into the very fiber of my womb and delivered to the hands of a loving God. I discovered that every moment matters to God. Even moments of despair brought me hope. And hope gave me the ability to lay my motherhood on the altar of surrender.

Surrendering our desires and our hearts to His will allows God to turn those seeds of trust into the fruit of His plan. He begins to grow our minds toward motherhood. When I surrendered my ideals, God grew a new and amazing desire and planted it within me. Full of passion and fervor, I discovered a love for what I was being called to and an understanding that every woman is given a mother's heart. We are asked to surrender ideals and embrace this high calling.

Women, we are called to be sowers.

Sowers. It sounds so mundane, doesn't it? Planting seeds, bending low, tilling the ground, sifting the dirt, pruning, watering, and weeding. It takes time and hard work to plant and reap a harvest. We need one another if we are to remember to continue to work with an end in sight, even when life seems fruitless or desperate. The heart and understanding we take into womanhood will affect our vision, our purpose, and our outcome. We don't need to suffer through God's calling on our lives.

Read that again. Motherhood is not a call to suffer through.

Motherhood matters because *you* matter. Your struggles matter, your questions matter, and your dreams matter. Embracing motherhood doesn't require you to give up the passions God has given to you. Motherhood does not destine us for drudgery and loneliness.

It is my prayer that you will find hope and help as we walk together through many motherhood matters. And that you will discover that *you* matter. Every woman has a mother's heart. A beautiful place from which we give, nurture, mentor, love, and dream. Let's grow those places together as we invest in others the gifts God has given us.

I wrote this book with every woman in mind. I sweep spilled Cheerios up off my floor, wipe runny noses, teach my children world geography, scrub toilets, change sheets, talk to my teens until wee hours of the night, manage sports and academia, and mentor my family every day, all day. Here you will find a thousand glorious mistakes and a thousand hallelujahs thanking the Lord that His mercies are new every morning. I don't hide the daily cracks and cries of my motherhood, because when we are broken together, we are in comm*union* together. Poured out.

We have a divine purpose and the plan has already been laid out for us. Every word, action, decision, and every training moment is a part of that plan. Everything has a why. Even motherhood. It has not been lost on our feelings of inadequacy, fears of failure, or drudgeries in the mundane.

Go easy on yourself, mama. God has the big picture. And let me tell you, it is a mighty beautiful thing to behold!

Part I

{WHY}
You Are Not Alone

*Love is heroic when compelled to be, the rest of the time
it is quiet and unrewarded, every hour on the hour.*

JOHN D. BLASE

1

{WHY}
Everyone Else Is Having a Baby and I'm Not

Motherhood was never a dream of mine.

I didn't play with baby dolls or talk about love and marriage, and I never once thought about having a baby of my own. I was the smiling, friendly girl in school who awkwardly dressed like the teacher and created seasonal bulletin boards for my bedroom walls. I listened to eighties music, learned and practiced all the current dance moves, lived on my roller skates, and sold Girl Scout cookies. I just never dreamed about motherhood.

That is, until the day I met my builder.

When we married during college, our thoughts turned toward the future. Our future. Did we want a family right away? We soon discovered that God had a bigger plan. Too many times my womb washed away any new hope I had of becoming a mother. Repeated miscarriages brought reality quickly into focus: There are no guarantees. The day we heard the first faint heartbeat, our hope, once invested in what was lost, seemed to come into focus and settle on something new. Life.

I Was Going to Be a Mother

We were counting the weeks to our long-awaited ultrasound appointment and confirming the new life growing inside me. The waiting room had limited seating that day. I was guessing the woman to my left was as far along in her pregnancy as myself, give or take a few weeks, and the woman to my right must've been there for a different women's health issue. She didn't pick up the assorted pregnancy and baby magazines stacked on the table in front of us, and she avoided the waiting-room chatter among the women about their due dates. I sat between these women awkwardly, as still as possible, a habit born of necessity, because any drastic movement threatened to heave my insides out and make my head spin until I passed out. Salted crackers and sips of water hadn't cut the nausea, and broken blood vessels around my eyes displayed evidence of my rounds of severe vomiting.

No one ever told me that motherhood would look like this.

It was in the middle of one of those fainting spells when our phone rang. "The doctor has a few concerns." Without further explanation or any assurances, the assistant requested that I return for an ultrasound.

So there I was. Called back to the exam room but feeling just as awkward and uncomfortable as I had in the waiting room, and even more isolated in my own skin because of the curt bedside manner and the sterile physical surroundings common in those days. The cool gel they applied to my stomach sent our little girl into a somersault. I watched in wonder as her petite features appeared on the screen and the sound of her beating heart filled the room. I could count the beats; they seemed in sync with my own. Her heart matched my own rhythm—steady, strong, and full of life. Seeing and hearing the big picture was enough to give me the courage to wait for the doctor's report.

I had grown to love this little babe that I had already carried for 20 weeks strong. It took a few months for me to relinquish the fear that this pregnancy might also end in a miscarriage; but her body was growing into mine, and I knew she was going to be the first little girl we would hold in our arms.

The doctor asked me to "clean up" and meet him in his office when I was ready. *What did that even mean?* I was a shaking, emotional mess in that room all by myself. As I sat on the chair in the corner and slowly redressed, I thought about how the next five minutes might go. The techs are trained to not convey any emotion or indicate whether something might be wrong. It took every ounce of my willpower to turn the handle on the changing-room door and step into the hallway leading to the doctor's consultation office.

Motherhood never felt so lonely.

Our doctor was in his last year before retirement. During his practice, he had likely been through this numerous times before. Yet I sensed hesitancy in his movement and noticed a hint of sadness in his eyes. The irony of the human heart played around in my mind. Here I was feeling sorry for this man who was preparing to deliver the most difficult news to me about my baby.

My concern for him disappeared when he not-so-gently handed me the death sentence for our baby in the form of a note to return to the office once we had made a decision. Basically, he gave us the choice to terminate the life of our growing baby or give birth to our little girl who had no kidneys.

I will always remember this as the first moment I ever questioned why.

The waiting room felt a lot different to me on the way out that day. I walked straight through a sea of happy, pregnant women with hearts full of hope, anticipating answers like, "It's a girl," and I headed home with more questions than answers. Right at the top of my list was the question why.

Nothing in the following few days made sense to me. I felt as if someone had pulled my heart straight out of my chest, and I saw the world through a veil of bitterness and confusion. The universe continued with joy and celebration while the builder and I felt as if we had to say good-bye once again to our dream of having a baby.

Why would God ask me to bury a dream again? Doesn't God want the best for us? I wallowed in the whys. I grieved over the whys. My baby continued to grow and to move, and I carried my dream close to my heart every day.

My body grew into motherhood, just like any other expectant mama—except, I was going to say good-bye and not get to mother her at all. How was I to let go of something I wanted while it continued to grow inside of me?

And then, one day, the builder and I were introduced to a couple who had experienced similar loss, and our lives were forever changed. We cried over our baby girl that day as they held us tight and prayed and so gently shared their wisdom with us. "Let God use this. Let

Him have your baby girl and let others see what He can do with broken dreams."

Maybe I wasn't meant to be a mother, I thought. *Maybe I couldn't be the mother God would want me to be.* When we despair against God's ultimate plan, we lose moments of blessing that could be ours—and more importantly His—while we grieve. Grief should not close our eyes to the work God is doing in and around us. Slowly and surely, God was opening my eyes to the possibilities.

Why would God ask me to bury a dream again? Doesn't God want the best for us?

For the last five months of my pregnancy I carried my little one with every ounce of love I had, knowing this would be our only time on earth together. If God was going to give me a gift, I wasn't going to complain it wasn't the gift I wanted.

I sang her to sleep and read her my favorite books. I went for walks and stayed up all night with her as she kicked and let me know that this was our nighttime together alone. I wouldn't have missed it for the world. She knew my heart from inside my womb, and she knew my voice—as she still does in heaven.

God gave me a heart for motherhood because He had so much more ahead for me to love.

Motherhood Captured Me at the Release

Twenty-eight hours of bearing down and finding strength from places within I never knew existed. It was the first life-giving sacrifice I have ever given. The burning, back-breaking pain of moving a breech baby down the birth canal and into the world forever etched a physical memory on my body. Manipulating with precise and skilled hands, our doctor reached for our baby's horizontal arms and moved them inside my womb to bring her bottom side out, painfully tearing the very part of me that I thought made me a mother. Pain control was not available, and the builder told me that my eyes pleaded mercy while his prayers begged for it to end.

The final declaration of my limited strength was my last pleading cry before my full-term beautiful baby girl was set on my chest. There she was, so perfectly beautiful. Her shallow breathing contrasted my own as my body exhaled the end of the struggle. Relief and relinquish was the call now. Her paper-thin fingernails, deep brown eyes, and curly, soft wisps of hair are forever etched on my heart. Her scent of heaven, the softness of her skin on mine, and her quietness are my very first memories of motherhood.

Capture and release.

As the physical struggle lessened, the emotional pull was gaining momentum. We knew that our firstborn was in a fight for her life. Her breaths were quiet, but her eyes spoke volumes. It was the most precious hello and the hardest good-bye.

The supernatural strength a mother has when she is captured by His grace overwhelms the release to come.

Watching your child take her last breath, while you hold her to your breast, leaves you empty on the inside for a very long time. The hands on the clock do not seem in sync with the years. Suddenly you realize that you may be losing time in the lost moments, rather than gaining gifts, as they pass you by.

Releasing Pain to Hold on to Beauty

Motherhood rushes past many of us and leaves us wondering if there is more. So much release and so little time to capture. The beauty of a woman usually has deep roots formed by the release. The struggle brings her to a place of confidence in her calling, but it is etched on her heart. The places that once held the hurt and the ache are now filled with mercy and grace. If we choose to let the moments make us and not break us, motherhood leaves an imprint of beauty, even when brokenness formed us.

A woman with empty arms is even more capable of grasping that which God brings her way to behold. We will walk through deep valleys and stand high on mountaintops. But without walking through the long, deep places of release, our view from up high would never be the same.

God reaches into the deep places of our lives and shines His purpose. Right down from heaven, He sends hope for the hurting mamas who tell Him, "I just don't want to do this anymore." It is okay to give up the fight and embrace the calling.

Waiting Expectantly for God's Go

Motherhood leaves an imprint of beauty, even when brokenness formed us.

The day we buried our beautiful brown-eyed, brown-haired little girl, was the day God showed me His dreams never die.

In our times of loss, we are called to wait expectantly on God. Grace and hope enable our 180-degree turnaround in the moments when we feel that enough is enough. Enough brokenness. Enough surrender. Enough of nothing to hold on to. The point of no return is where everything can be turned around.

When our motherhood is calling us to leave something behind or say good-bye to dreams in our hearts, we are not giving something up. We are giving something over and waiting on the Lord to return an investment from our sacrifice. Often we consider the turn in the road to be an obstacle.

Truth to Live By

The Lord is my strength and my shield;
my heart trusts in him, and he helps me.
My heart leaps for joy, and with my song I praise him.
(Psalm 28:7 NIV)

God does not place obstacles along our way to His plan. We might view waiting as a roadblock rather than the slow walk to the green light He already has purposed. Motherhood may feel like a sprint, but it is a slow, careful run to the biggest victory plan ever. Roadblocks and defeat will surely come, but He wants us to come forth as gold.

Taking the Steps

You may be the woman who is waiting for God to answer your prayers for motherhood and the wait is wearing you thin. Maybe you are up to your elbows in mothering and you are wondering if you are ever going to see the other side of the dream. The wall between you and your desires has taken on the banner of maternal desperation.

Take a step back from your circumstances long enough to see the beginning, and remember that the end is in God's hands. Look beyond the emotion and the sacrifice to feel something new in your bones. Follow the unfamiliar tug at your heart to leave the grief and the weary ache behind. That will require true sacrifice, as will answering the call to pick up where you left off with a renewed sense of commitment and appeal.

Do not be discouraged by the release of your dreams. God wants to first capture your heart, and His firm grip will hold you tightly enough to bring all those pieces together.

Motherhood captures us with a grip of commitment—with the call to be willing to release. Do not lose heart or let go too soon. The waiting is the mystery. The giving is the gift.

My Parenting Principle

Motherhood is never a guarantee, but a woman who waits with an expectant heart will always reap a blessing. As I wait upon the Lord in my motherhood, I release my will to His and do my best to capture the moments He has for me as His plan unfolds. In every moment I give back to the Lord, my motherhood is being perfected so I can finish this race. God will not bury my dreams, and He will allow beauty to grow out of the ashes.

Abba Father, I am leaning into You as I feel the weight of these words and the brokenness in my spirit. My arms feel empty and I ache for the dreams that are not birthed yet. I bring my own heart and the hearts of my friends who walk through dark valleys and struggle with the release. Fill me with Your presence, Lord. I seek Your face and Your peace, as I wait in deep surrender. You captured my heart, and I am releasing my plan to You. In Jesus' name, amen.

2

{WHY}
Dreams Are Never Really Buried, and Faith Is Resurrected

Buying a dress for your baby's funeral is something that's not supposed to happen.

My husband and I grieved together and had to push into the unthinkable right away. I wish I had known my breasts would still react to the maternal call, preparing milk for my babe, still quite tender to the touch. This was how my body called for my child. My empty arms longed for her. My painful stitches from her breech delivery were another constant reminder of what I had lost. Through the physical and emotional anguish, it was torture to shop for something, anything that might fit my tightly bound chest and postpartum body.

As the builder pushed me in a wheelchair through the stores, we were met with smiling, sympathetic faces. Shopping for Elisabeth's funeral brought a public eye to the space I wished to keep so very private. The builder and I would just look at one another in the mirror of the crowded changing room as he helped me change from one uncomfortable dress to another. We would pause and hold one another shaking our heads in disbelief and pain at what was to come.

On the rainy October day of the funeral, hundreds of people gathered to honor the life of our baby girl. It is surreal to sit in the front of a church knowing that the tiny white casket we had so carefully chosen held our sweet babe. A forever good-bye from a front-seat pew.

I never knew that saying good-bye would take so much out of me.

Barely able to stand at the cemetery while our friend played "It Is Well with My Soul" on his cello, I wept with deep ache over what was to come. It felt like a cruel twist of a dream. As we said good-bye to the tiny white casket, they carried me away with arms underneath mine. I was unable to stand the pain of knowing I was leaving my baby at the cemetery. I knew our Elisabeth was in heaven. I knew God's arms were holding her tight, but my arms were empty, and this was all I would feel for a very long time.

I thought I had buried my dream of motherhood on that rainy fall day. As they placed her in the ground, my heart sank to the lowest of places I think it has ever been. Alone. With nothing to show for my pain but grief.

Six months later, my heart was nearly broken when my body surrendered yet another baby to heaven. My faith in God calling me to be a mother was tinier than a mustard seed, and I began to unfold the why of motherhood with God every single day.

When Pain Births a New Focus

The beautiful thing about God's plan is that it is infinitely bigger than we can see. When we put our faith and trust in a Savior who died and rose for us, we can have reassurance that He never left us, even when part of us feels as if it's gone.

My faith in God calling me to be a mother was tinier than a mustard seed, and I began to unfold the why of motherhood with God every single day.

I spent my days alone playing the piano, making meals for my neighbors, attending bittersweet baby showers, and celebrating life all around me. Although I thought my arms were empty, the Lord was filling me up from the inside out.

I began to see the people in doctors' offices differently. I would drive by the cemetery and watch others grieve, and I couldn't get through one single hymn without tears of healing from understanding what those words meant. The whole world came into a new, sharp focus.

I realized, during this very quiet time in my life, that every woman has a heart of compassion and caring. A heart to protect and nurture others' dreams and a spirit of fortitude to encourage and see the needs of those around us with new eyes. A woman will sacrifice her own body, health, spirit, and dreams for another person. Why? To be the life-giver to another person, in the womb or out, in word or in deed, and in their prayers to the ultimate Giver and Comforter of all.

Truth to Live By

He comforts us in all our troubles so that we can comfort others. When they are troubled, we will be able to give them the same comfort God has given us.
(2 Corinthians 1:4 NLT)

Even when everyone else was having a baby, and I wasn't, God had given me a heart to mother. My faith found a resting place, and I began to lay down my cross in surrender. It was a pruning like no other. While I gave Him my plans, He grafted new fruit into a barren place, and I would see that fruit someday in the future. While I let the bitterness go, He planted a desire to embrace the new plans He had for my life. When I uprooted the fear of loss, God planted trust in a Holy Plan.

We do not need to suffer great loss to realize that God has a great plan for our lives. We need to embrace the hope that His plan is perfect, and surrender our own. It is then, and only then, that He can use us completely. The Lord and I had many long, hard talks. I fought the lies that whispered doubt, and I poured myself into being used by Him.

It was humbling to realize that motherhood is my poured-out offering and not just a gift of receiving. He was sanctifying me from the very beginning, even when I never dreamed of being a mother; it was His plan all along. While every bit of us holds onto hope for a blessing in motherhood, it becomes a spiritual journey of giving back and letting go.

? free — will

I'm conflicted
I don't believe God plans out terrible events.
I think we choose to continue to have faith despite those terrible things.

Motherhood matters, because you matter. He created you for this.

Walking Together in the Empty Places

We began this book at the most empty of places any mother could find herself. The letting go of her child, her dreams. The release is almost unbearable, and although you may not be walking the road of grief, I can promise you that someday the very heart of your motherhood, which captured you from the beginning, will leave you. Here we will begin the journey of preparing. Learning to walk with those who need us and understanding that our investment today will be the reward of the release in our tomorrow.

Lonely. Empty. Angry. Depressed. These are just a few words to describe how women feel when they have lost a child or cannot carry a baby.

We walk through a spiritual wilderness in those empty places. Infertility, miscarriage, and loss usher us to the loneliest places a woman may find herself. There are deep crevices along this journey that only God can fill and cover with His mercy, grace, and comfort. I would encourage and challenge every woman to learn how to minister, and be ministered to, during such days or years. It is our call, as sisters in Christ and mothers alike, to walk with other women and to speak life and truth from His Word. We are called to accompany them through this valley of death—death to dreams and death to life. Let's use this place to call ourselves up and into a new place. A place where we are confident this pain is not to be ignored, where it's not awkward or shameful to talk about, deal with, and find comfort in. We need one another. So let's begin here.

Taking the Steps

Explore these questions when you can take a bit of time to reflect on your answers.

1. Are there dreams you have had to let go of or say good-bye to? Take some time to list those dreams and see if your heart has truly healed over those losses over time. No

matter whether a dream is big or small, we might still
mourn it. ~~Dream of having~~ Dream of parenting my kids
with my mother. Reveling daily in their lives and musing
over every action, word, a deed.

2. Do you have a friend who is walking through loss? Think
   of women in your life who have lost a baby or may never
   be able to carry their own. How can you come alongside
   them? Have you ever asked them to share their story with
   you? How do you respond to this difficult time in a friend's
   life, and how can you walk with them through it?

   when friends post their grief on facebook

3. Have you shared your story of loss with someone else? If so,
   what happened when you did? Have you come to a place
   where you feel God has healed this empty space so you can
   minister into another woman's life?

4. Are you afraid to talk about the release? The pain, the
   emotion, and the struggle? If so, why?

5. Did you feel inadequate to comfort another woman in the release of her dreams?

Motherhood may capture us, but the release of dreams, loss, or our children of any age is a painful yet natural part of our growth in Christ. We need to share our losses, our stories, and let the words bleed surrender and healing as we talk and listen. Let's break down the barriers of loneliness, shame, and isolation in our losses and be the audience God deserves. We have to begin somewhere. Let's stand with one another and in the gap of the empty places where we may be hurting.

My Parenting Principle

I will recognize everyone has a different story and a different outcome. My broken dreams can be redeemed when I allow my pain to comfort another. Every woman has a mother's heart. I will be intentional to use the gifts God has given me to mentor, comfort, encourage others. Motherhood is for every woman who embraces her calling to nurture and feed her soul and pour it out into others.

God, it is with open hands I pray today. Every day brings a new surrender and release of the pain and disappointment I have held on to. Will You use me for Your glory? Will You take this vessel and allow me to be filled with Your peace so it overflows into the lives around me? I seek Your comfort and strength in the days when my anger or sadness overtakes me. Help me be victorious in this place. I trust You, Lord. In Jesus' name, amen.

3

{WHY}
Overwhelmed Does Not Have to Be Your Middle Name

I don't know why every epiphany I have needs to be preceded by an emotional roller coaster; defeated shoulders slinking into a hot, lavender bubble bath; and my mind reeling from mounting stress. I tell myself how overworked, overwhelmed, overwrought with emotion I am, and how unfitting I am to be anyone's mother!

This is when I realize the very thing I needed to do before the breakdown even began—at the point when it is too late to prevent the falling apart, the defeat. When will I learn how to avoid those overwhelming moments that seem to suffocate me while casting doubt and fear over the purpose and vision I know I was created for?

I need to hear this on repeat: <u>Fill my cup before it is empty</u>.

When I was in the thick of my early days of motherhood, it didn't take a lot to pile on levels of stress that seemed insurmountable. As our quiver grew in number, my overwhelmed state came from a mountain of laundry, projects, lessons, correction, schoolwork, and the list goes on, as you may know quite well yourself. There never seemed to be an end in sight. My work and my worth felt the weight of my new reality. I was in over my head, and I wasn't counting on finding my way out anytime soon.

Overwhelmed had become my middle name. It was clearly written all over my life, and I had no clue what to do about it. No one came alongside me and suggested I take a step back. No one gave me practical advice on how motherhood, in all its glory, didn't need to be such a pit of despair. I was living in survival mode, and you may be also. But may I please appeal to you, right here in this moment? If you are not this woman, you most likely know someone who is. This is your opportunity to be an answer of prayer to the mother who loves her children but may not necessarily be liking motherhood right now. Reach out. She may not be waving her white flag of surrender where you can see it. She may be so buried in her stress and responsibilities that she cannot even reach her hand out from under it all to wave for help.

Women Are Called to Be Seekers

Why do we wait to feel overwhelmed before we do something about it? Women tend to put others' needs before their own, and in the end, it backfires, causing us to resent our investment and the tiresome result. We talked earlier about being sowers, but God has also called us to be seekers. We are to be intentional in noticing and reaching out to the other women in our lives. We all have opportunities, every day, to reach into another woman's life and hold her up while she works to regain her footing.

Those of us who are feeling a little relief or perhaps have learned something along the way, well, we should be offering up a hand, a heart, a word or two to give that other mama a bit of relief and confidence in her calling. I like to call this the "no-judgement call." Where women feel safe in reaching out and reaching in, knowing we have all been there, done that, and not one of us will ever claim to have attained perfection.

And if you need to be on the receiving end of help, wave your white flag high for help. Raise it, wave it, and ask. We are called to ask for help. There should be no shame in the plea. Your *overwhelmed* is God's opportunity to amaze you. Let Him fill your cup so you can overflow into another woman's life just the same. I want you to know the peace that can come at the end of the longest day motherhood will ever throw at you.

Daily Stretches Make Firm Habits

So what can a woman do when she feels her stress reaching disproportionate levels, or when she has resigned herself to thinking that this is "just the way it is"?

Yes, you will feel tired. You will feel lonely. You will feel stretched. This is the reality of it. Each phase of mothering is always replaced with a new season. We are relieved when our babies sleep through the night, and then we are shocked to find out that our teenagers are craving long discussions late into the evening hours and robbing us of our now routine bedtime. It is a never-ending cycle of sacrifice and stretching.

But you don't have to be overwhelmed all by yourself. It's time to turn off the noise of the world and tune back into what matters. You *can* do this and it *does* matter. Turn away from the noise and clutter—the habits that make you feel so defeated.

Often we lose sight of the root of our stress and find ourselves caught in the perpetual cycle of putting a Band-Aid on the symptoms. When we pull the sliver out of a festering problem, the pain seems more bearable. Let's figure this out together.

Your *overwhelmed* is God's opportunity to amaze you. Let Him fill your cup so you can overflow into another woman's life just the same.

I have discovered that although I am a quick learner, my habits are not strong right out of the gate. Learning to be patient is the first required lesson before we tackle being overwhelmed. When you begin tearing down the things that are bearing weight against you, there will be a lot of stretching and learning going on. But the best is yet to come. Daily lessons in motherhood grow into life habits of teaching. So be careful what you are practicing. Growing pains will birth new life in you and your home. Someday we will look back on our seasons of struggle and be thankful we allowed them to grow us and not overtake us.

Pushing Points and Our Overwhelming Responses

"I am done." When you hear yourself say this, it is past time to make some changes. Don't put it off any longer. Here are some other clues to help you discern whether you are carrying the weight of your worries.

1. You begin to raise your voice and lose control of your emotions in response to your situations or the pile-up of responsibilities at home.

2. You are not getting enough sleep.

3. Your children do not bring you joy any more. You find yourself complaining or sighing when you spend time with them or need to do something for them.

4. You have stopped taking care of yourself.

5. Your marriage and relationships are beginning to suffer, or you find yourself in conflict with others more regularly.

6. You are feeling inadequate, lonely, or desperate for help.

7. You cannot get a handle on your job, your emotions, or your thoughts.

8. Home is not a happy place anymore. You are aching for an escape.

Throwing Off Every Weight

Perhaps by now you have realized that it's very normal to find yourself in this place of defeat or being overwhelmed. You may have even asked yourself once or twice why motherhood even matters, when you are feeling like such a failure some days. Just today, I drove my car in tears as my son's behavior brought all those same emotions rushing back to my heart and mind, and I had to take a few minutes in a parking lot to throw off the heavy weight of it all. I succumbed to the emotion, asking myself when I was going to figure this whole thing out.

Truth to Live By
Give all your worries and cares to God,
for he cares about you
(1 Peter 5:7 NLT)

The unnecessary load we carry, thinking we need to be on top of every little thing or have an answer and a solution to every motherhood matter, will weigh us down into a continuous cycle of defeat.

Our Thoughts Dictate Our Responses

It is time to throw off lies the Enemy uses against us and claim the truth God desires to clothe us with. Do not be burdened with thoughts never intended for motherhood.

What does this look like in the everyday life of a mom? Remember, practice takes patience and a repetitive motion of remembering our purpose. When I find myself in this pit, I begin with my thoughts. I remind myself of these truths, over and over, speaking life into my bones and my heart.

Life-Speaking Truths

1. God created me and has equipped me for this purpose.
2. I will not believe lies based on the emotions of my circumstances in the moment.
3. There are truths in the Word and from other women I need to remember right now.
4. I will put off the negative response and put on loving thoughts.
5. God has a unique plan for this circumstance, and though I may not know what it is, I will respond with an open mind and let emotions take a backseat until I can respond correctly.
6. My heart is too tender to handle this hurt or the weight of

all that is before me. I will choose to see this problem as small and God as big.

7. The big picture cannot be lost on everything before me.

8. I will begin with one new habit today that will break this situation into smaller manageable tasks.

9. What will I put off today and tomorrow, to find a balance between what is expected and what is needed?

10. Have I reached out for advice, help, or care when I need it?

11. What will my one new habit be per week to help me find myself at peace with my motherhood?

12. What is pushing my buttons—the list of things I need to do, or my inability to find a way out from around it?

Taking the Steps

When our minds are fixed on the truth, everything else comes into focus. What we do with our focus dictates our outcome. We can choose to only see our mountains of stress, laundry, work, schedules, deadlines, and everything a woman is asked to do, or we can deliberately make that 180-degree grace turnaround and look toward faith. It all begins with recognizing our point of focus and determining if it matches our motherhood vision. Let's have a conversation to process a few things you might be feeling.

Am I the only woman feeling as if she's dropping the ball? I cannot keep up with everything I want to do or is expected of me.

You are not alone. Have you found a small space of quiet for yourself yet, to sift through your priorities, your purpose, and your schedule? What can you let go and what is the root of your excess?

How do other women manage everything and still find time to fit in the extras?

You are not other women. Remember, God has given you the very minutes and hours in your day. You can choose to follow a schedule that brings everything back to your purpose in motherhood. Anything outside of this is extra. Motherhood does not have to be mundane. Be sure you are enjoying the choices you have made.

Will my emotions ever feel normal again?

Consider the season you are in right now. Emotions are not something to be afraid of; it's what we do with them that matters. Every season will bring a new scope of feelings or responses. Go easy on yourself and take one day at a time, back to a new normal. Your grief, your overwhelmed feelings, your loneliness will not be forever. Take hold of hope. Give yourself the self-care and soul-care you may need.

My Parenting Principle

God has equipped me for motherhood. I need to utilize His resources. I will begin the practice of putting on His armor every day, remembering my purpose and not allowing a privilege to grow into a burden.

God, I am on overload with everything motherhood is expecting of me right now. I will be honest and say that I am not enjoying this season, and I am left wondering if it will ever end. I am seeking Your help and strength to be patient in the process. Help me, Lord, to practice putting off the negative thoughts and putting on Your truth. Will You infuse me with the big picture in my parenting and help me to find peace as I work to make better decisions and handle my responses differently? I need more of You and less of me right now and every day. I give this day to You and every minute of tomorrow. Help me to walk in grace. In Jesus' name, amen.

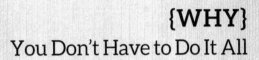

4

{WHY}
You Don't Have to Do It All

With my back to the bathroom wall, I sat on the cool tile in the dark and thought about how much I wanted to get up, head out the door, and walk away from it all. My husband, my kids. All of it. Everything that meant stress, responsibility, and more of me given to everyone else. The desperation in my bones was ruining me and rushing at me like a wildfire. I needed to flee.

I was going to escape. I had my clothes packed into a small, green suitcase, the keys in my hand, and not even the tiniest plans for my next step. While my baby and the builder slept in the other room, I cried tears of emptiness and brokenness that were lost in the night. It was God and me on that bathroom floor as I threw my motherhood at His feet and desperately told Him I couldn't do this anymore.

It was crazy. Crazy, I tell you. I had a baby, toddlers, teens, and my builder husband, who worked ridiculous hours and had no idea that the tears, the pleas, the complaining, and the begging to help me find my place would mean that I was going to walk away from it all— this beautiful life that any woman would give her right arm for and probably would shame me for feeling so ungrateful about. But those women weren't raising this brood on a shoestring, working from morning till night with a baby at her breast for fifteen years, fulfilling all the expected roles at church, and...the list continued as I laid it all out in my mind on that bathroom floor. Desperately seeking relief, I felt as if the next thing I would lose would be my mind, if I didn't flee now.

There is nothing lower than lying prostrate in your tears and asking

God to make it all go away. The only thing we can focus on when we get this low is the urgent need to find the answer.

I can see how women get to this point. And I cast no judgement. Because in those moments, all judgement is gone. While I remained nearly lifeless on the bathroom floor, crying all my tears dry and pleading with God to show me the way, everything became clear. My purpose had become lost on my day-to-day living and I had traded it for a pile of problems. I had it all wrong. Somewhere along the way, I thought that I needed to be doing "it all."

This moment escalated into an undiagnosed health problem. I spent Mother's Day in the hospital, hooked up to IVs , with my nursing baby sleeping beside me. My children having to visit me in the hospital on Mother's Day is a memory I would rather forget. But it was a monumental moment in my life when I finally understood that motherhood trumps anything extra that might be calling my name, and that I needed to let other women into my life to help me.

I had traded my purpose for a pile of problems.

My awareness of my reality and the plea of my heart for help opened my eyes to the race I had been running without a purpose. Motherhood had become my 24/7 job, and I had become robotic in the motions and movements while leaving my heart and my focus behind.

Know Your Purpose

I will always vividly remember this time in my life as if it happened yesterday. The passion that was born out of this brokenness drives me to champion other women and encourage them to stay focused, stop picking up more to do, and to know their purpose. To know their big why.

Look what I had done. God had become small and I had become the hero to my family and to everyone else. You can only do this for so long, for you will fall and you will fail.

God's voice was loud and clear to me the night I was ready to turn everything in for sanity and identity. The very life I was living was all

I needed if I was to refine and restore the most fulfilling season of my life. I just needed to repurpose my vision to meet my every day. And you can too.

Truth to Live By

As the deer pants for the water brooks,
So pants my soul for You, O God.
My soul thirsts for God, for the living God.
(Psalm 42:1-2 NKJV)

It took a few years to repurpose my life, to retrain my daily schedule, my priorities, my response to stress, and to choose to see the goodness in my calling. It was an intentional pursuit that revolutionized my motherhood and gave me back my joy and identity in Christ.

Let It Go

How do we sift through our emotional and physical lives and hold on to what's important, yet, let go of what's bogging us down? Can a woman be everything to everyone and still know her purpose and identity?

We beat ourselves up every day over a to-do list, others' expectations, and self-inflicted superstar status that takes God off the altar of our hearts and replaces Him with "woe is me." Often we find ourselves waiting for permission to remove some of our tasks from the "responsibility" column to the "it can wait," or "unnecessary" column.

Have you picked up more than you can handle? Remember, you are not the woman next door. Her calling will never be yours, and your lives will never look the same. Remember that things are not always what they seem. She has stressors like you do; her circumstances just look different from the outside.

It is a backbreaking habit to carry around expectancy and a load of unnecessary work. It is also heart-wrenching to know that some things cannot easily be let go. This is your life. So what is going to give? Well, we know it will not be your children or a spouse, or all the love, care, and investment we pour into them. They are at the top of the list. Right?

Maybe we have mixed up our desires with their needs. Perhaps that is how and where we have lost sight of our purpose.

When you say no to the right things, every good thing comes into focus. Finding your way back from being overwhelmed will take daily practice and pursuit.

Choosing Between Good, Better, and Best

There are a lot of people vying for your attention and a whole lot of appealing projects you would love to add to your to-do list. I get it. I am a visionary, and my mind never stops moving ahead of my daily responsibilities and priorities. Your full calendar may give you a shot of adrenaline as you see all the good things you are investing in and the activities that will keep your family happy. Your life may be so full of long, sleepless nights and extra loads of laundry, you wonder how any woman has time for a hot cup of coffee.

When you say no to the right things, every good thing comes into focus.

Our seasons will never look the same as someone else's seasons. It will take a concerted effort to sift through the good choices, the better ones, and finally, your best options. It may take overcoming a feeling of guilt when you cannot do what others expect of you, or learning to humbly ask for help to find this balance.

If you understand your purpose, it's easier to set boundaries. I have gathered a few ideas to help you choose what may be best. Add these four words to every decision process you make. Write them out, memorize them, and filter your choices, your thoughts, and your scheduled priorities through these four simple measures of how a decision serves your purpose and God's purpose for you.

Accountability: Does this choice follow God's Word and a trusted mentor's wisdom?

Timing: Can something new fit into the bigger and best picture?

Vision: Am I making choices that align with my vision and purpose?

Focus: Am I remaining steadfast in keeping top priorities and valuable investments first in thought and action?

Women always put others first. Therefore, the struggle is real when deciding which choice might be best for us, best for our family, or best for both. This takes practice, but the sanity at the end of a long day of good choices is worth the effort.

Taking the Steps

Have you figured out your pushing points and emotional responses to life's situations yet? We need to take time to study ourselves and know how God made us uniquely. We can avoid the stress of a long, emotional day by avoiding the triggers we know put us into a bad frame of mind. Take time to identify the exact moments, stressors, or circumstances that cause an emotional reaction in your life.

We cannot avoid life, so a better plan is to read, study, and understand how God would wish us to respond. How can we meet those moments *with* Him, instead of pleading with Him after it is too late? Skim the list below each day for a week and see how you might incorporate these new perspectives and practices into your life.

Daily Practices to Become Less Overwhelmed and More Amazed

Before you put your feet on the floor in the morning, pray and keep praying.

Make your bed. Make it pretty.

Give yourself permission to enjoy the moments, rather than seeing everything as a task.

Act; don't react.

Take something off your to-do list that can wait.

Go for a walk, even if you need to take your children.

Get in the Word. Get your family in the Word.

If you do nothing else: Rest and love your family.

Tell your family how much you love them. Don't just show them.

Find one spot and moment for quiet time and free time. Guilt free!

Always bring moments back to the Lord. Even spilled cereal.

Celebrate your wins and shake off your mistakes.

Give yourself grace and prayer time to make the big decisions.

Claim God's truth over the lies you may hear.

Memorize one verse a day. Write it on your heart.

Smile. Let your family see you smile.

Let your *no* stand on its own. You don't need to list all the reasons you've declined.

Give someone the blessing of helping you.

Put your family first, even when it comes to ministry opportunities.

Avoid lumping all your problems, to-do lists, and responsibilities into one emotional pile.

My Parenting Principle

My motivation for doing all things should always come back to the purpose God has set before me. Anything else will always feel like a burden. I will continue to view my choices and my activities through a lens of the healthy, the positive, the necessary, and things of eternal value. My personal life and my motherhood can hold beauty, creativity, and the freedom to say no to those things that are causing me added stress and burden. I will learn to manage my life with healthy boundaries, without minimizing my motherhood in the process. I want to be fully present with my children and not fighting stress when externals may be vying for my attention.

Dear God, Sometimes I wonder if I will ever learn this lesson. Over and over I take on new things, only to find myself pros-trate before You laying them back at Your feet. Will You help me to be filled with peace as I live every day with intentional choices? I am so tired of thinking I need to do it all. Help me not to compare myself to others or live in doubt over my calling to motherhood. I will trust that Your plan is for me to grow in the place I am planted right now, and it will lead me to free-dom in finding my identity in You.. You are my everything,

and I ask You to forgive me for always putting You last. Help my eyes to stay on You and my vision to stay focused on those things You have for me right now. I am often discontent, and my mind wanders to bigger, more exciting things. As the hymn says, "Bind my wandering heart to Thee." In Jesus' name, amen.

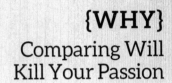

5

{WHY}
Comparing Will Kill Your Passion

Two years ago, I sat on the edge of the local pool in the heat of the summer and had a conversation with another mother that transformed my life. She asked me why I was not attending the local mom group events. Little did she know that the answer to this question had long been a source of sadness in me. And it was something I had never told anyone.

I had never been invited.

Yet I am what seems like a perfect candidate for a mom's group. I have ten children, ages 24 to 5, and even though I have adult children I am still in the thick of raising little ones. There is no doubt that I am a mom. But the events were by invitation only and I couldn't quite figure out how to insert my desire to be a "part of the group" without forcing myself upon a lot of younger moms. Don't we all need to be filled up so we can be poured out?

The craziest thing was that she didn't seem too surprised that I had not been invited. This was obviously a topic that had come up before. I sat quietly waiting for her response.

"September, I am not surprised about this. You intimidate other women."

And that was it.

Silence. Awkward silence. I wonder now how long I stood there with my mouth wide

Don't we all need to be filled up so we can be poured out?

open and my heart raw and flaming in embarrassment. I never thought of myself as intimidating. I was stunned.

And then it began: the shaky, sinking feeling in the pit of my stomach that seemed to be blocking any clear thought or audible response. After a long pause, I told her how sorry I was to hear this. And then I remembered what God had called me to speak into other women's lives.

We should never have to do motherhood alone.

I told her it was my prayer and desire that those women would take the time to get to know me. Really get to know me.

I share this story for one reason. Her words were the most truthful words spoken to me in a long time. My life *is* so very overwhelmingly full. It's even intimidating to me as I live it—some days I barely get by without locking myself in the van. I often end up talking out loud to the Lord to gain some perspective. I am the one intimidated by mothering to the masses. She was right.

This motherhood role can be overwhelming and sometimes so lonely. But because of a lack of communication and understanding, the women were intimidated by me rather than overwhelmed for me and with me. It took a while for me to realize that it required great honesty and bravery for this woman to speak those words to me. I am grateful to her.

I have used this as a reminder to stop and not be intimidated by my own life when I am in those moments of overwhelming motherhood. It helps me understand that every time I take on the full responsibility of raising my children well, I am taking the credit for what God has done, is doing, and will do.

Breaking the Cycle

For a whole year, I let the comparison with and from other women cause me to step away from everything I had become and doubt what I knew to be true of my womanhood. I began to make my circles smaller, and my words seemed to disappear. I began to doubt the gifts God had given to me. I began to focus on me and what I could do differently so I wouldn't intimidate other women. I began to fall out of step with my purpose and the holy pursuit that God had given me peace with.

Truth to Live By

Create in me a clean heart, O God,
And renew a steadfast spirit within me.
(Psalm 51:10 NKJV)

See what comparison had done?

Comparison is a trap laced with lies. It catches us off guard and ensnares us in a circle of doubt and negativity. We know what comparison feels like, looks like, and what it does to us. It is like an outfit we choose out of our closet that fits us to a tee, and we model it with such conventional dislike.

Yet would we recognize a genuine reach across the table, a message of help, and a note of encouragement for what it is? Or would we scrutinize it and second-guess the intentions behind such gestures? Perhaps we hide the real and the raw from other women, thinking that our junk and our exhaustion are better kept hidden.

Run from the entanglement of comparison.

I refuse to make motherhood about me. I refuse to compare myself to other women. I refuse to take the credit for what God is doing.

Comparison builds walls. We should build bridges.

Taking the Steps

Get to know the women around you. Give them your hand, your heart, and your honesty. Invite them in. Let's skim the overwhelming right off the top of the motherhood cup we fill every day, and be there for one another—before we are running on empty.

Drop your shields, raise your swords, and go forward with strength, into one another's lives. You do not need to feel overwhelmed when you have an army of women holding you up.

This unity and camaraderie is missing because we are afraid to let the world see that we need help, we need hope, and we need one another. Comparison keeps our true selves hidden, and it creates doubt, shame, and negativity. Motherhood should be a sisterhood and not a long-distance relationship.

We are sometimes oblivious to the barrier between the generations and the gaps that have caused women to not extend themselves into one another's lives. We can begin retraining our vision, our mind-set, and our daily practices in our relationships to connect, to encourage, and to gather.

My Parenting Principle

I am responsible for my own motherhood. I will embrace my differences, my children, and my calling—for them and for the Lord. I will encourage other women by coming alongside them and not creating a barrier of isolation because I envy them or I'm afraid of our differences. Fear will have no hold on me or my motherhood, and I will be the bridge that fills in the gap of relationships and understanding. My view of other women in their seasons will be purposefully filled with grace and understanding, and my words will relay my genuine care for them. I will not be intimidated by the trap of comparison. My heart needs to turn to a real and raw place and to see others—the way Christ sees me.

I refuse to
make motherhood
about me.
I refuse to
compare myself
to other women.
I refuse to
take the credit
for what
God is doing.

Father God, You have not given the spirit of fear. I need to shake the lies I have heard or I believe other women feel about me in my motherhood. Will You create in me a clean heart and allow me to see others as You see me? I do not want to feel uncomfortable in the presence of other women, because of the comparisons that run in our circles. Help me fight for the truth in this generation and the next. I want to believe the best for other mothers and let them know I am in their corner. Help me, Father, to be at peace with my own weakness and mistakes, that I may be able to be honest and humble when I can learn from others. Help me to shine more of You and allow these traps and lies to not weigh me down anymore. In Jesus' name, amen.

6

{WHY}
We Need to Let Them In

There it was again. A soft knock on my screen door.

I was hoping it wasn't so. Of all the times to have visitors, why did it have to be now? I had chosen this day to relax. I had six kiddos under the age of nine still in their pajamas at one in the afternoon, and a home that held a few piles of unfolded laundry on the couch, a nursing babe on my breast, and a table left sticky from a PB&J lunch. We had gone apple picking the day before, and the over-achiever in me seemed to rear its head. In hindsight, we had picked way too many! There they were, those beautiful, shiny apples in bags on my kitchen floor, causing a little more than an overwhelming picture to my life. I had chosen to be present with my kids today and now it seemed to be backfiring on me.

Walking to the door, I smoothed my fingers through my little girl's hair, pushed a few toys aside with my feet, brushed the crumbs from the tabletop to the floor, and opened the door with a hesitant smile. I was greeted with the warmest of faces and the gentlest of eyes in a woman 30 years my senior. Her speckled, gray hair was neatly combed, a stark contrast to my postpartum body, and I immediately felt small, defensive, and hesitant.

I didn't move from the door. I was secretly hoping she was just dropping something off. But her cheerful words told me differently. She was just dropping in for a visit, and I was mortified to let her in. I always had my home in order, clean and running smoothly, but this day, this single day, I had chosen to let it all go for some rest and downtime with the kids. It was time to eat humble pie.

This day changed my life. Forever.

This dear woman walked into my home and never once did she look around. She kept her eyes on me the whole time. She sat at the table with her arms carefully arranged around the sticky leftovers and she held my baby with so much love. She didn't look at the dishes in my sink or the mountain of laundry unfolded on the couch. She carried on the most pleasant of conversations, ever so gracefully ignoring my inner turmoil and anxiety over every little thing. She let the kids crawl onto her lap and she read them books. She asked me how I was and what I would be doing that week.

Truth to Live By

Hope does not put us to shame, because God's love has been poured out into our hearts through the Holy Spirit, who has been given to us.
(Romans 5:5 NIV)

I was a bundle of nerves. I skittered around like a maniac for the first ten minutes, offering her refreshment, washing a glass in case she said yes, and ridiculously trying to make everything perfect. She never blinked or acted annoyed. She smiled and told me she just wanted to visit with me. And never once did she bring up the dishes or comment on the state of my disarray for that day. She could have offered to help with the mess but she knew me well enough to know that I had that under control and that the offer could easily be an offense. Instead of piling on guilt or triggering embarrassment, she was perfectly present to put my heart and mind at ease. She sat right there in the sea of craziness and beamed like a lighthouse I wanted to draw near for comfort and security. I wanted her peace, and she was bringing it to me.

I had been waiting for her to point out my motherhood imperfections, my messy corners, and that obviously my children were still in their pj's at one in the afternoon. That never happened. She was just there to meet me where I was. This was the first time another woman had ever overlooked everything else and put value in just me. It was a glorious unfolding of the perfect picture of sisterhood in the thick of the mess. A sanctuary of blessing that every woman should receive.

As she stood to leave, she kissed my children, and I remember seeing them look up into her deep eyes with adoration; I knew they would never forget her. There was another dart of conviction to my heart. I had worried so much about the state of my home and my appearance that I didn't recognize the full gift God was extending to me and to my kids. This awakening was a mighty strong and beautiful thing.

When she got to the door, she paused with a brief hesitancy (insert the Holy Spirit working here) and sweetly turned to me and said, "I see you have some apples there that need to be finished into applesauce." After a long, awkward pause on my part, I quickly told her about our eagerness while picking and the joy it brought the kids to see their hard work in number. But she and I both knew half of those apples would never make it to the freezer or the canning jars. That was the truth of it. She had quietly noticed those apples earlier, but upon leaving, told me that she would love to take them home so she and her retired husband could sit and peel, core, cook down, and crank out our sauce like no tomorrow. As a matter of fact, it would be fun for them. Go figure. My job would be fun for her. Or at least, that's how she put it. Because she knew my pride might get in the way and I might say no.

Oh, that moment was so defining. With all my heart, I knew it was the right thing to let her take those apples. It was a true gift, but with all my pride-filled emotional reasoning, I wanted to tell her that I was good. That we were going to make it a family project and it would be fun. But, I knew that it would be all me. All stress and all regret if I didn't let someone help me.

Those bushels and bushels of apples went home with my friend with sparkly eyes and sprinkled grey hair. A few days later, she returned the finished applesauce to my home.

The Humble Act of Receiving

As soon as I opened my door and let her into my world, my friend showed me the beauty in just being there. Her presence and joy was exactly what I needed that day. She was wise enough to know I didn't need to be fixed or tidied up on the outside. She filled those deep cracks that I had hoped to fill with a down day and more.

Just let others in. Let women into your life to fill the cracks and empty places with hope, help, and a faith that cannot be shaken even in the hardest of your motherhood days. Let them in.

It is so much easier to give help than to receive it, isn't it? This is the crux of the breaking point, where we, as women, make the most humbling of choices. When we receive with open arms, we will be filled with the fullest of blessings.

Let women into your life to fill the cracks and empty places with hope, help, and a faith that cannot be shaken even in the hardest of your motherhood days.

When we are inwardly drawing a line and keeping those private, overwhelmed places a secret, we will always be bound to our pride. It's like a wall of refusal. We are telling others, God, and most importantly ourselves that we've got this. We don't need anyone or anything else. What will we be left with? Ourselves and our mess. These things will create new walls in relationships and our hearts—walls that are hard to break down once erected.

Taking the Steps

It takes practice to receive well. It's a daily giving back to the Lord and a lesson in learning how to let others into our lives. When other women are showing us genuine love and concern, we can differentiate between them and those without good intentions. Discernment is key, but not a tool to lock away our loneliness and need for help.

The biggest first step for any woman is to let others in. But where do we go from there? How does this look in real life and off the page? Here are a few simple questions to ask yourself to determine what letting others in might look like for you.

For the Younger Mothers

1. What is keeping you from reaching out for help or allowing someone to be a part of the messy parts of your life? Write those things down in the space provided.

2. When women begin to draw closer and ask questions, do you shy away or put up walls? If so, why?

3. Do you feel that the older generation may judge you or meet you with condemnation rather than grace in their efforts to be helpful?

4. Have you experienced the sweet blessing of another woman coming alongside you and lending a hand? If you have, how did that make you feel? If not, who can you turn to for help and fellowship?

For the Older Mother

1. Are you able to put your own ideas and judgements aside to walk with another mother in grace and patience? If not, what's holding you back? If so, what can you do differently?

2. Do you ever feel that you "have done your time," and this generation can figure it out just like you had to? What does this generation need that fits what God has prepared you to give?

3. Have you felt a resistance or a wall from the younger

generations that perhaps they do not need or want what you might have to offer? What was that like?

4. What would be a practical, grace-filled way for you to let other women know you are there for them?

My Parenting Principle

We are called to live life together. God created us for community, and my motherhood can be enriched when I let others in. I will pray for God to send grace givers and wise women to walk through motherhood with me. May I remember the wisdom and experience available to me when I let the older generation into my life. Motherhood can bridge the gap in the generations, and I can be the hand and heart to extend this invitation.

Lord, why do I complain about my loneliness, my workload, and my weariness, but raise my banner of independence so high? Help me see my need for external help and hope. Will You give me the courage to invite others into my life who can invest and be blessed in return? I have been stubborn and so full of pride in trying to hide my weaknesses and my needs before others. I confess those empty spaces need to be filled with the women You have placed in my life for this part of my motherhood. I give You control, and I will make steps to let them in. Help me to be brave and receive well. In Jesus' name, amen.

Let's Talk

Dear friend, you are so loved. It is my hope and prayer that you are fully convinced you should never have to do motherhood alone. Even in your quietest moments, you are not alone.

Loneliness is the number one response many women give in their description of motherhood. Many of us don't have someone walking with us or ahead of us to lean on. I encourage you to find a handful of godly, wise women who are willing to come alongside you in prayer, encouragement, and edification.

Many days, when I consider the path God has chosen for me, I think I am unworthy of this calling. When motherhood gets hard or the journey seems to overwhelm me, I tend to crumble and hide. Life can be a tidal wave of emotion, and I often succumb to it. When we sit together like this and you are reading pages of my personal journey, I wish I could sit close and share more stories with you in person. And I wish I could hear your stories and hopes, too. There's always so much more going on in our lives than is evident from the outside, isn't there? It isn't until we share our journeys with one another that we understand all that God has done and is doing within our respective lives.

It is amazing to me, as I look back on my beginnings, to see how far God has brought me. Not from me attaining or achieving, but more of a bending low to let Him cover me with grace, letting my imperfections shine through. He has sifted me through and through. I believe this is why motherhood matters so much to me. It has been the most refining part of my life, and it has not been hidden from the public eye. Before you turn the pages here, I want you to know this about me. I am talking to you as a friend. I am not an expert or child psychologist.

Our lives may look different in so many ways, but motherhood is universal. It is a messy, hard, beautiful, and stretching (literally) journey, and I will not hide any of this from you. My words are not written to paint a picture of achievement or excellence, but to encourage you in the moments that matter, when you feel alone and unnoticed. I wrote these words for you and for me.

Our passions become our pursuits, and I am passionate about championing you and encouraging you to embrace motherhood, because it matters. You matter to me. Let's turn the pages with a new focus and a renewed energy.

If your heart is tender and you are wondering if your dream for your life will ever be birthed, I am here on bended knee, praying for all our broken places. Your life matters to God. He would never want us to live in regret, shame, loneliness, or the defeat of comparison. Is it hard to shake off the lies you have come to believe about your motherhood or your life?

When we sit together like this, we can be open and honest and real with one another. As you walked with me in my grief and loss, I want you to know that your empty places matter and God cares for you infinitely more than you could know.

I pray that the words in this book will usher hope into your heart and you will find the joy in embracing motherhood, so you will be able to thrive!

Part II

{WHY}
We Cannot Live Motherhood
by the Seat of Our Pants

For the mother is and must be, whether she knows it or not, the greatest, strongest and most lasting teacher her children have.

HANNAH WHITALL SMITH

7

{WHY}
We Can Learn to Love Our Children Uniquely

In between the craziness of mothering and managing this household, there's always a bit of conflict brewing that I need to address. Between school, music lessons, sports and work schedules, toddlers and teens, our personalities abound and attitudes arise. Some days are harder than others, and life can swing hard on days that seem to be the least convenient.

Opportunities to learn to love our children well often come knocking in the middle of a conflict. Sadly, conflicts might arrive when I miss a child's love language, or when reconciliation moments are lost in the busyness of life. Rather than lament over the reconciliation moments I'm missing, I have tried to more intentionally read my children's hearts, to learn their languages of love, and to meet them where they are. But then I miss a heartbeat, get busy, and conflict begins to brew. This became evident in a growing resistance from one of our children. We needed to address the problem.

There is a point in our motherhood when we realize the external behaviors our children exhibit are pointing straight to their hearts. Sometimes, it takes a little longer to sift through their unique personalities and wade through the conflicts to get to the heart of the matter. Add in our busy lives and distracted motherhood to the mix, and we're going to miss some potentially healing moments.

One of our busiest weeks brought this lesson to the forefront of our lives, when one of our children seemed to be at odds with every single person in our home. You know what I mean, don't you? They seem to be in the middle of every person's business, pushing buttons and throwing attitudes at you like they're wet noodles, hoping they'll stick. At first, I excused our daughter's behavior as a bad reaction to a heavy school load. Then I tagged the ups and downs as hormones. And when I didn't think it could get any rougher, I realized that my once extroverted child was now quietly moving through the motions of her day, and conflict seemed to be coming out of nowhere.

Love doesn't have a schedule, and our children's hearts never get the memo that we are doing our best, but there will be gaps in our attention. This just so happened to be the case with my preteen girl and her tender heart.

Truth to Live By

Love from the center of who you are.
(Romans 12:9 MSG)

Life had taken over, and I was missing the learning curve to her heart. This particular summer week, with our busy schedules and errands, I had not found a moment to give our home or hearts the attention they needed. Yet the moment I returned home one morning with a trail of groceries and children behind me, I was met with a surprise: the house had never looked so spotless. It was a glorious reentry during a hectic morning. The bathroom was cleaned top to bottom and every cupboard in the kitchen had been emptied out, organized, and meticulously put back together. Someone had been busy, and I took notice. But before I could find out who to thank, the chaos of putting the groceries into the pantry, a knock at the door, a brief, unexpected visit from a neighbor, and the necessary pursuit of the runaway fowl, distracted me from my course. Before I knew it, it was time for me to begin preparing dinner. Conflict always meets us full in the face when we wait too long to meet the heart. Dinner hour was going to bring a heart-to-heart, face-to-face meeting with love and our girl.

While I would've preferred to have enjoyed our mealtime with laughter and easy conversation, I asked questions of this child about the attitude she was sporting, trying to figure out who she was upset with, why, and if she was aware of her outrageous behavior all week.

A stare was her sullen response. I could have pushed and prodded. I could have set off a few tears by digging to get to the bottom of the dark mood, but something in my mother's heart told me to just wait. I calmly communicated that her heart needed some searching and pointed out that there had not been evidence of love for her family this week.

The normal dinner routine of manners, table talk, passing the water pitchers, and listening to the tales from everyone's day continued, until I noticed the silence that had set in at this child's corner of the long family table. She is not a quiet child by nature, yet now the stinky attitude had been replaced with a quiet sadness. The builder noticed it too. We exchanged concerned glances and an unspoken agreement to get to the heart of the matter. This child asked to be excused from the table, but we asked her to stay. I knew it was time to pull back the layers of frustration and agitation she was carrying and address the core issue before another moment passed.

Always trying to ask questions and not accuse, we found ourselves unsure how to reach her heart when she was so hesitant to respond to our inquiries about her lack of respect and love lately. But then, after another long silence, she spoke words I will always remember: "Why doesn't anyone think I love them? I show them all the time. All week I have been doing things around the house and no one has taken notice. You say I have a bad attitude, but I don't understand why you can't see all the things I do, because *I love you*."

Her words struck me to the core.

Instantly my mind replayed all the ways our daughter had *shown* her love. It all made sense now: The mail retrieved every afternoon, the groceries carried in, the floor-to-ceiling cleaning! All these efforts and details had been her way of saying that she loves us, and all the while, she had waited with longing—and eventually with hurt and disappointment—to hear the same words back.

I love you. *Acts of service.*

Her love was there all the time. She was waiting for me to show her how much I appreciated everything she did, and I had missed the opportunities. When we aren't in tune with how our kids individually give and receive love, we will miss their efforts and their needs. The more aware we are of our child's love language, their personal and unique way of giving and receiving love, the easier it will be to notice and give love in return, even in the busiest of our motherhood days.

Our aim in motherhood is not to raise a cookie-cutter image of our likeness with our interests and the personality traits that suit us best. We do not want to raise a robot child, whose only aim when they grow up is to please us and to live under the pressure of meeting the standards of love that we might expect. God gave us children with unique abilities and sensitivities and ways to express themselves. That is something to celebrate and honor!

> Our aim in motherhood is not to raise a cookie-cutter image of our likeness with our interests and the personality traits that suit us best.

Speaking Your Child's Love Language

Finding your children's strengths and love languages is like mining for gold. While you are panning and sifting to find their gifts and talents and help them grow, you discover the way to their hearts.

All hearts speak a love language. If you cannot speak their love language, how will they hear you? Often when children are asked why they love their mothers or how they know their mothers love them, their answer will key you in to their language of love!

"I love my mom because *she hugs me.*"

"I love my mom because *she takes me to baseball practice.*"

"I know my mom loves me because *she tells me.*"

Can you hear the language of love in each of the above responses?

In Gary Chapman's encouraging and insightful book *The 5 Love Languages of Children,* he identifies five particular ways that people might experience love from others. Here, I will briefly describe those languages to help you begin the process of exploring the love languages your children understand.

1. Physical Touch and Closeness

Physical touch often speaks louder than words. This would be the child who would let you hold her all day, or asks you to hold her wherever you may be. He loves it when you rub his forehead or his back or hold his hand on every walk into the grocery store and while you are helping with his schoolwork. This child smiles at you when you are sitting close to her at the table, or hugs mean more to her than a bowl of ice cream.

2. Words of Encouragement or Affirmation

The word *encourage* means to "instill courage." There is a difference between affection and praise. We show affection and love to express appreciation to our child for the way God made him or her. We praise a child for something she has done.

The child who speaks this love language will light up like a sunbeam when told that her cursive is awesome, that his bed was made the best, or that she will do great at the play auditions. He will interpret your measure of love for him by your words rather than your time, your touch, or your gifts. None of these other expressions will have the same impact as your words of encouragement, gratitude, and positive conversation.

We also need to understand the impact negative, harsh, and cutting words will have on this child. The greatest enemy to words of encouragement is *anger*. Our volume and tone of voice has great influence over a child's reaction. Positive verbal affirmation speaks volumes of love.

3. Quality Time

This language requires focused attention. Time spent doing most anything with this child will be perceived as love, whether you sit on the couch to have an attentive, intimate conversation or hang out as a family in the living room with everyone doing something different. Wash dishes together, go for a walk, read a book to him, or plan a family game night. Make eye contact with her when you are together. It isn't about fitting in or forcing these moments, but focusing on building them into your shared experience with this child.

Truth to Live By

Love is patient, love is kind. It does not envy, it does not boast, it is not proud. It does not dishonor others, it is not self-seeking, it is not easily angered, it keeps no record of wrongs. Love does not delight in evil but rejoices with the truth. It always protects, always trusts, always hopes, always perseveres. Love never fails.
(1 Corinthians 13:4-8 NIV)

When a child's primary love language is quality time, and her love tank is empty, she will go to any length to get it. Even negative attention seems better than no attention to this child. It is not the event itself that is important to the child, but the time you are spending with him. You can provide focused attention anywhere. Be careful of the trap that we may fall into as parents when we have children who crave quality time. Our time with our children should not hinge on whether their behavior is pleasing to us or if they deserved this attention. Love is unconditional, and the time spent with quality-time children should not be taken away as a punishment or because it is inconvenient for our schedules. Quality time requires intentional sacrifice. This is how we show them love.

4. Gift Giving

Generosity will define this love language. Your child will be a happy giver and receiver of even the simplest of gifts.

You may have a child who would give you his favorite stuffed animal, or a teen who would give her last five dollars to the homeless person on the corner. This child may buy gifts for every single person in the home at Christmas and will stretch his savings to make it work. Gift givers are easy to spot, since they are generous and appreciative. Little things, gifts, and tokens of love go a long way with gift givers.

It's important to remember that this love language is not natural for all of us and can be easily overlooked. Often it is confused with bribery, since parents may find it easier to buy something for their children rather than an intentional message of love given with their gifts. Often a handwritten note or a token of love left in his or her room will go a long way. We should be careful not to attach a price tag to this love, and to meet our children's hearts uniquely where they are. This will require a sincere effort to know your child well.

There is a common misinterpretation of ungratefulness in a child who does not give or receive love through gift giving. You may find yourself shocked at the reactions, or lack thereof, from children who do not value gifts as others do. Such times give you an opportunity to discover more about how your child *does* experience love.

5. Acts of Service

This child will be eager to help out. He will run errands for you, be the first to step into a needed role, and volunteer for the smallest details that you may not want to ask for help with. She is generous with her time to serve others and usually does so with a joyful spirit. She will love to serve with you. And this is the best opportunity to show these children Christ's love in action. They are the next world changers—the feet and hands of Christ.

We all know that acts of service can be emotionally and physically exhausting. A word of caution with this love language: Be careful not to use this language to limit your children. Begin by helping them do things they cannot do for themselves. Move toward creating independence by showing them how to serve others or when they need help. Don't force extreme independence on them.

How to Discover Your Child's Primary Love Language

1. Observe how your child expresses love to you.

2. Observe how your child expresses love to others.

3. Listen to what your child requests most often.

4. Notice what your child most frequently complains about.

5. Give your child a choice between two options.[1]

Our homes can and will be different places when we go straight to the heart of the way God created each of us. The most important thing to remember is that you are doing the best you can. The point is not to re-create yourself or your children, but to draw out their strengths and to strengthen their areas of weakness. And the balance in all of this? We become better lovers, better givers, and better receivers; and our children can know and see that we really, truly love them, because they see us trying.

At the end of a long day or a full-fledged fail at loving your kids well, these words might be the very thing you to need to play, say, text, or write out, on repeat: "I love you. I'm committed to you. I care about you because you are my child. I don't always like what you do, but I will love you no matter what."

Taking the Steps

Have you identified your child's love language? Don't forget to identify your own. This will help you see how you give and receive love as well. Here are a few questions for you to consider as you evaluate the changes you may be considering:

1. Is there a child in my home or already grown who I struggle to understand?

2. Do I have a disconnection in communication or understanding with one of my children that is disruptive to our home?

3. Have I taken the time to invest in speaking my child's love language, or do I find it difficult to embrace those differences?

4. Am I missing out on receiving my child's love because I am waiting expectantly for my own needs to be met?

My Parenting Principle

Love is not always easy. It requires sacrifice. I will love my children as individuals and not just "members of this family." I will commit to seek the gold that makes that heart shine bright in the unique way God has made my child. I will learn to speak his or her language of love and be a better receiver.

Dear Lord, I am desperate to know my child's heart. I seek it every day, but I feel as if I am missing something. Will You give me the wisdom and the understanding to see and know my child's language of love? I trust in Your promises that we should train up our children in the way they should go, and they will not depart from it (Proverbs 22:6). I am seeking You and Your face today, asking for help to hear my children when they show or tell love and give clues to how I can love them uniquely. You are love and love casts out all fear. I need You now as I give this everything I have. In Jesus' name, amen.

8

WHY}
Your Children Can Learn to Love One Another Well

They sat on the leather sofa watching me with disbelief as I tied their hands together with a sock. Honestly, it was all I could find, and it was conveniently stuffed in the couch cushions. It seemed appropriate at the time. I think any onlooker would have thought that I had lost my mind. A desperate parent will pull no stops when we are over-the-edge tired of hearing our children quarrel. There they sat, hands tied together, inching their bodies as far away from one another as the stretch in the sock would allow. I was so tired I had to turn my back to the kids as my stern look of anger gave way to a smile and I had to squelch my laughter at the scene playing out in front of me.

Maybe in some psychology book there is a term to describe what I was doing. I'm not sure. But it was my last resort to make a point. And it did. We had a long talk while their hands were tied together. Their angry eyes began to soften and the slight curl of a smile emerged at the edges of their lips. Always a good sign. If peace had to come like this, then I was willing to try it. After all, the Bible says, "Blessed are the peacemakers: for they will be called children of God" (Matthew 5:9 NIV). And if parents aren't peacemakers, I don't know *what* we are!

Did my children argue, squabble, or have conflict after this? Of course they did. The sock incident only changed the direction of that morning; it didn't change their hearts. And so, over the years, I realized that my children need to understand and learn one big lesson: Love begins in the home. If you cannot love your family well, then how will you love others?

This point of discovery was where my mission began: Find a way to train my children to love, and show them what love looks like.

I can remember the moment in my motherhood when I realized the lessons of love had settled into my children's hearts. Be warned, mothers: Love has no boundaries and will not fail. When you pursue this in your home, do not be surprised at how powerful love can be. It's a gift you are not only giving your children but also the world as you prepare to launch those arrows into society.

Love begins in the home. If you cannot love your family well, then how will you love others?

When Correction Inspires Courage

One hot summer Sunday afternoon, when we were all together and life's routine seemed to settle on us with happiness, our children chose to engage in foolish behavior. In such moments I wonder what in the world is going through those young minds and hearts. We had seen so much progress with loving, peacemaking, and relationship building, and now it seemed as if we had taken ten steps backwards. But sometimes we all need to back up a little before we can gain perspective about moving forward.

Correction is my least favorite part of motherhood. So this parenting day tore up my heart like no other. But I know we all require correction in our lives if we are to grow and learn.

The builder lined up the six oldest children, ages 5 to 14, in a straight row facing us so we could ask them questions about the incident and get honest answers. It didn't start off too well. The youngest, who is known for her dramatic personality, was in a tizzy, and we decided that she should just sit quietly; pulling anything sensible out of her was going to be a true miracle. The oldest three stood in solidarity. It was a sight—almost as if the bickering between them hadn't just happened five minutes earlier. They went from a country divided to an army united; they were going to stick to the same story.

I knew we weren't headed for a good ending if someone didn't confess. I think every family has an Honest Abe. Our truth girl had a conscience speaking to her, and she stepped forward from the line to tell us what happened. Now every eye was downcast in shame and every child remorseful over his or her behavior. The truth was out.

We heard the story—the long and the short and the in-between. The stories all matched their remorse. The truth teller stood quietly now, with tears streaming down her bronzed summer cheeks. My heart wanted to say, "It will be ok," but I knew this behavior needed correction.

Two brave feet stepped out of the line and beyond the edges of sibling toes. The owner of those feet, my son, quietly and boldly told the builder he wanted to take the correction for his truth-telling sister.

My heart exploded. This love. The very love I had been teaching and talking about and trying to give them during those frustrating years stood tall in front of me.

Two more feet shuffled forward. This time they belonged to the oldest of the bunch. I will never forget the look of conviction on his face. He spoke with a resolution of love to take the correction for every one of his siblings. All the love right there in that line broke me. I was now the bawling, sniffling dramatic mama who had to leave the room.

What Does Love Look Like?

Love stands tall. Love will always trump conflict.

You can raise children who love one another well, but they should know what love is and what it looks like. Don't expect them to just wake up one day and know. It takes work that will require plenty of sweat and tears from you. Your heart will ache as you see their different personalities clash and the conflict that ensues when they cannot put their own agendas aside.

Love cannot reside where selfishness is rooted.

Motherhood has so many intentional moments, but pulling the root of selfishness up and out in your home is one of the hardest, most painful jobs there is.

Not one of us enjoys hearing we are selfish. Not me, not you, and especially not our children. Moms seem to get the bad rap when it comes to addressing the hard stuff. We just want to be the good guys that have a happy-go-lucky friendship with our children. Some days it seems that every time I open my mouth to speak to one of my children, I am correcting, edifying, explaining, or questioning their behavior.

Love stands tall.
Love will always
trump conflict.

Does any of this matter? Are they even listening?

The day my sons stood tall and stepped forward, I saw the reaping from the sowing. The weariness was replaced with a knowing that all those words, those talks, the uprooting of selfishness had made a small impact on their future.

Never give up on loving your children. Love wins every time. Why not begin at home?

> ### Truth to Live By
>
> Jesus replied: "'Love the Lord your God with all your heart and with all your soul and with all your mind.' This is the first and greatest commandment."
> (Matthew 22:37-38 NIV)

Change the Atmosphere of Your Home

It often will take us by surprise. We notice negativity, conflict, or a pervading atmosphere of unsettled emotions, and we wonder, *Where in the world did this come from?* Mothers have the power to shift and stabilize the atmosphere of their families and can turn a day right side up or upside down. We often don't realize the impact we have as mothers in the home, until the home may be out of control. Women can ignite happiness, spark anger, diffuse arguments, and lift the fog of discouragement in any atmosphere. Mothers are mood makers, and it is our job to set the tone in the lives of those we are given to steward. It may seem daunting, but it is truly a gift. Don't feel as if it's a huge weight of responsibility or something you are required to do. Your home will become who you are, and your family will shine forth this atmosphere wherever they go. What does this look like?

Be the Change

1. Be in the Word of God daily.
2. Overflow with the goodness God gives you.
3. Fill your home with music, art, literature, and fun.
4. Smile.
5. Discourage arguing and complaining.
6. Avoid gossip and don't be a Debbie Downer.
7. Keep a schedule and spend time together.
8. Learn to love one another well.
9. Be creative and fill your home with laughter.
10. Don't allow the hardship of the world to stain or discourage your conversations.

Speak and Model Peace, Not Conflict

Like it or not, we are the runway models for godly or good behavior in our homes. Our family and those who know us are our audience. We often overlook the influence of our own tongue in the home. Our words influence the steps of resolution we take or don't take to work through a conflict. It is possible to have a home that permeates peace. Many families consider yelling, avoiding others when there is a problem, keeping an emotional distance in relationships, and many other symptoms of a broken love, to be "normal." Mothers, imagine the power over the nations, the generations, if you are willing to model and speak peace into the very fiber of your home and your children. It will be life changing.

> You were taught, with regard to your former way of life, to put off your old self, which is being corrupted by its deceitful desires; to be made new in the attitude of your minds; and to put on the new self, created to be like God in true righteousness and holiness.

Therefore each of you must put off falsehood and speak truthfully to your neighbor, for we are all members of one body. "In your anger do not sin": Do not let the sun go down while you are still angry, and do not give the devil a foothold. Anyone who has been stealing must steal no longer, but must work, doing something useful with their own hands, that they may have something to share with those in need.

Do not let any unwholesome talk come out of your mouths, but only what is helpful for building others up according to their needs, that it may benefit those who listen. And do not grieve the Holy Spirit of God, with whom you were sealed for the day of redemption. Get rid of all bitterness, rage and anger, brawling and slander, along with every form of malice. Be kind and compassionate to one another, forgiving each other, just as in Christ God forgave you (Ephesians 4:22-32).

How We Can Communicate

It's easy to lose sight of the ship when the fog rolls in. I remind myself of this when life overtakes me and I cannot figure out how I found myself trying to diffuse sibling rivalry or handle a conflict that festered with my teenager way too long. If someone could just help me navigate through this muddy time, I think, it would all go away. But conflict can be just under the surface and will pull us under if we don't learn how to navigate through it. All relationships take work and time. We have applied very basic and biblical rules to the communication in our home, and they have helped us walk through some serious issues and discussions that would have been much easier to avoid and let fester.

Four Family Rules to Better Communication

1. Be honest

2. Keep current—don't focus on the past

3. Attack the problem, not the person

4. Act—don't react

Foster Sibling Love, Not Rivalry

With the varying personalities in our home, I am a very busy mama working to foster love and not rivalry. I spend a lot of time encouraging, teaching, and reinforcing the fruit of the Spirit, and I find less and less conflict when we all work harder to grow God's fruit in our lives. All mothers desire their children to love one another and to do it well.

Truth to Live By

Instead, speaking the truth in love, we will grow to become in every respect the mature body of him who is the head, that is, Christ. From him the whole body, joined and held together by every supporting ligament, grows and builds itself up in love, as each part does its work.
(Ephesians 4:15-16 NIV)

The thing is, our children cannot love if they don't understand what love looks like in a day, in the middle of a conflict, or when they do not care for the actions of their siblings. It's our job to teach them every day how to put on patience, kindness, and self-control. It is possible to raise children who have healthy relationships with their siblings.

It may seem daunting, but the daily practice of fostering and growing love and grace in your home will usurp the devastating effects of ignorance over what might seem to be a small matter.

Encourage Honor and Respect

There is no better way to raise children who love one another well than to teach and model true respect and honor toward others. Imagine the possibilities in our homes if we were to treat one another with only the two words here:

Honor: to show appreciation, respect, or affection for

Respect: to think very highly or favorably of

Honor and respect have been lost on the busy, fast paced, me-first world that rushes through our revolving doors and our fluid schedules. The importance of putting others first requires the act of putting on true humility daily.

Taking the Steps

I know exactly what some of you may be thinking right now. *It would take a miracle to have one day of peace in this home.* If just one day is all you are asking, then, let's begin there and consider the steps we can take to get the ball rolling.

It's important to prepare helpful and practical ideas that will pull your family together when the struggle to step away is real. Here are some ideas our family turns to when we have a new concept, plan, or an important matter we all need to discuss. Try putting them into practice as you plan your one day of peace:

1. Have a family meeting. Seriously, this is a real thing. Your family will most likely laugh at you the first time you call for a meeting as a group, but you will walk away hooked. It might take time for everyone to loosen up and get used to the idea of sharing their ideas and emotions as a group, but this is where honesty and trust grows in all of you.

2. Introduce the four rules of communication to your family and explain that they will be your "go to" for every word or conversation that you speak to one another.

3. Talk about what the Bible speaks about love. For example: "Love is patient" (1 Corinthians 13:4 NIV). Take one attribute or action like this from the Bible, and have everyone practice it every day for one week. At the end of the week, ask, "Were we patient to one another this week? How and when?" Be sure to praise good behavior and character. Then move onto the next attribute.

4. Discuss how to handle conflict. Cover the principle

that we are responsible for our own words, actions, and reactions.

My Parenting Principle

I am raising the next generation. It is important for me to consider the relationships my children have with one another as the groundwork and practice for any future relationship they will have as adults. I will commit to pursuing unity and fostering honor, love, and respect in my home now. This is their future, and I will parent with this focus in mind.

God, You have given me this family to love, and yet I feel as if we are missing that very thing. I want the arguing, fighting, and conflict to end, but I have no idea why my family won't listen to me. I am asking for confidence to share these ideas with my family. Will You prepare their hearts and minds ahead of time? I know Your plan for the family is to love as You love us, but even I fall short with loving You. I need Your daily reminders to encourage my children in love, so they will learn from my example. In Jesus' name, amen.

9

WHY}
You Should Love Your Spouse More Than Your Kids

The silence was so heavy it pressed on my heart like a vise. I would sit at the dinner table and inwardly fume at the imperfections I felt existed in the man at the head of our table. Hearing him rise and leave in the morning turned to relief for me. It gave my mind a break from evaluating the reasons we weren't seeing eye to eye or why our time together often turned into conflict.

Was I falling out of love with the man I pledged my life to? Was he getting the leftovers after my full motherhood days?

No one told me that I could have such lonely, silent times in a marriage. What happened to the days that seemed so bright and beautiful and filled with such promise? I didn't know that the arguments would be heartbreaking and our selfishness would loom in front of me as I washed dishes or folded the laundry, cared for my babes, and lived life as "the wife and the mama."

My loneliness, the disagreements, and even the love that we had shared together, seemed to slowly fade into busy lives caring for children—lives filled with exhaustion, short fuses, and a weariness that would cause us both to ignore the problem or give up altogether. After we said "I do," life happened, and children took up residence in the cracks of every inch of our life. My role as a mother seemed to completely take over. Until there was (almost) nothing left to the man and wife that God joined together from the beginning of time.

I had become the mother. He had become the father. And we had lost us.

Truth to Live By

Do two people walk hand in hand
if they aren't going to the same place?
(Amos 3:3 MSG)

When did motherhood take priority over my marriage? Like a thief in the night, it stole parts of my heart without my realizing. Motherhood can be demanding. It is no wonder we lose our first focus of love and give our children everything we have.

Turn Your Heart Back to Your First Love

My heart took a very slow turn one evening when I was pressing garlic into the soup crock and heard the front door open and close with the rhythm I knew to be my man's arrival. I could hear the familiar sounds of him sitting on the steps in the foyer to untie the long, dusty laces that kept the heavy boots on his feet all day while he hammered and lifted and built. His sighs and the moan as he stretched his tired body to rise from the steps to wash up for dinner sent a tingle of familiarity through my bones.

Had this been yesterday, I would have walked into the other room to avoid conversation or any approach of his presence. But this very night, God was moving in my spirit, and I waited at the stove. He walked slowly from the sink, and the scent of lumber, sun, and air was fresh in his passing. I never knew that the sun had a scent until I loved for the first time. God gave me a builder. A craftsman, working with his hands and with the elements that I grew to love as much as I loved my man. But falling out of love didn't take away this memory. It was another monumental moment, softening my heart.

I can't take one ounce of credit for what God was doing in moments like those. He was chipping away at my hardened love. Some people might look back and think we were a mess, and they would be so right. I wish someone had come alongside us to lovingly tell us that parenting is not a priority over marriage. It takes a lot of love to make a home, but our spouse deserves the firstfruits.

You cannot really fall out of love. You just need to figure out when you began loving something else more. Your love is like a strong cord and it can never break or go away. We had just let go of the rope, or let it uncoil to the ground in a loose pile. The pull and strain of life, babies, work, financial stress, and marriage can shear away at the strands of the love you have with your spouse until there seems to be nothing left to hold onto.

But the love that God joins together cannot be broken. Once my eyes were opened to the love I had lavishly poured out onto my children and withheld from my husband, I knew we had a lot of adjustments to make in our home. I learned the hard way. Don't let motherhood get in the way of your commitment to your spouse.

I see it every day. Mothers love furiously and forget that their husbands came first.

Fight furiously for the love of your life. Motherhood comes second.

> You cannot really fall out of love. You just need to figure out when you began loving something else more.

Even When You Think You Are Right

If there is anything I am sure of, during or after a conflict with my builder, it is this: I am right. Why can't he just see, come around to my side of the issue, or listen more? I'm being sarcastic, of course. The detangling of an argument should never take place in a heated moment. Our reasoning is far from clear when we are fully distracted by anger, loneliness, busy children, and feeling the strong emotions that come with any motherhood badge.

Remember that it takes two people to maintain a loving relationship; and when one of you has checked out, or placed a diagnosis on the other, then only one of you is actively working to solve the problem. Handing out a prescription to the love of your life or maintaining a haughty, lonely stance will only leave you feeling empty and alone. When we remove ourselves from any ownership in a feeling of separation, we are standing alone in our problem.

Your Children Need You, But Not That Much

The day the builder looked me in the eyes and told me he needed me more than I needed him was the day I realized what I had done. I had created an idol out of my motherhood. I'd been giving, giving, giving to my kids, from the moment they were in my womb until the present. They were my everything. I had shifted most of my attention and time to the service and caregiving of my children—to their present, their future, their comfort, and their success. I was still present as a wife. I still loved my man, and I was committed to making our home the very best I could *for* him, but not *with* him. Not with his hand in mine, together. We were working toward the same goal as two separate entities rather than two people who formed one force, one purpose.

It happens slowly. You cannot place blame on love and devotion for your children. Don't be too hard on yourself for giving every ounce of your flesh, blood, sweat, and tears for your family. But maybe step back and take a larger, wider look at the direction of your attention in the big picture. Where does your spouse fit into your planning, your passions, your priorities, and your big family purpose? When your focus is only on motherhood, you can and will sideline your spouse.

When your focus is only on motherhood, you can and will sideline your spouse.

Unintentionally, we draw closer to our children than our spouses. When we spend every waking minute potty-training, comforting their boo-boos, or learning their love language, why wouldn't our hearts be drawn in?

After 27 years of marriage, I have discovered that my truest of heroes and the man who fights for my motherhood more than anyone is my builder. He has seen the sacrifice and he has surrendered the most of any of us. He waited for me to come around to the other side of the deep breath that took me away from his focus for a time. Some marriages never make the mend after the rip at the seams of parenting. I have friends nursing the torn pieces of their hearts and marriages right now after raising a family together. It happens easily. But we have this time, right now, to learn from others and to cheer for victory for the institution of marriage that God set up for human beings.

Hold on to your love. Find it again if you need to, and learn to love the new you. Your marriage is worth fighting for, and the effort you sow into the strongest cords of love will be the very fiber that holds you together from this day forward. Your children are waiting for you to model love, remember? Don't wait another minute to find your way back.

Truth to Live By
Finally, all of you, be like-minded, be sympathetic, love one another, be compassionate and humble.
(1 Peter 3:8 NIV)

Where to Go From Here

When we realize how much we have let go of, we may begin to blame ourselves for missing the moments that we can never replace. You did the best you could in the time you had. You would be considered a superhero if you had finely balanced the impact of pregnancy, body changes, feedings, hormones, lack of sleep, and every little thing that grows on us when we take on motherhood. We are discovering the new person we are becoming while growing old with a man who is watching this craziness from the other side of the bed. It is probably just as confusing to him as it is to you!

While we and our spouses fumble along in this new, expanding life with respective fears and uncertainties, it's easy to start on separate paths. The thing is this: We can grow *with* one another, rather than going our different ways, handling our ever-growing families, bodies, and budgets alone. We were created to do this together.

Taking the Steps

When the builder and I became a true team, the change was evident to our children. It drastically changed our parenting and our model of loving. If there is one word to clearly define the instrument of our beginnings together, our restart, it is this: *humility*.

A woman who has found imbalance in her relationships can always go back to where her love is being given. It is normal for a woman to feel that maternal sacrifice and pull, but when her priorities and her heart become misplaced, then her life will feel empty. Loving both God and her spouse will take intentionality.

Every one of us is inclined to lose sight of that which is most important in our lives. Often those things that matter the most to us get in the way of our first loves. The builder and I created this list to keep us in check when we find ourselves feeling separated by distractions. As you go through your day, answer the questions and take the action steps. Soon you will notice the difference, and so will your kids.

Loving Together Checklist

1. Am I functioning off my own to-do lists daily?
2. Have we lost our vision as a couple?
3. Kiss every day. In front of the children.
4. Do we communicate about our needs and desires more than business as usual?
5. Are we working as a team in our parenting?
6. Go to bed together at the same time.
7. Always say I'm sorry in current time.
8. Remember that we are both changing. Learn to love the new.
9. Never stop talking.
10. Be available to each other at all times.

My Parenting Principle

God gave me two first loves. He is my spiritual first love and my husband is my earthly first love. My children are a blessing for me to steward and raise together with my first loves. I will turn my heart back to my first loves and commit to making daily investments into us. My motherhood is a beautiful gift birthed from our unity. I will learn to love my spouse for who God created him to be for me.

How did this happen, Lord? I felt the rift, the tear in my heart, and I have been blaming my husband this whole time. Lord, even if he does have things he can work on, I am asking You to give me a fresh spirit of desire for my man so I can love as You love me. Will You re-create my thoughts, helping me to keep him ever before me when I make decisions or spend my time? Thank You, Lord, for creating a helpmeet for me. You are my first love, and I want to go after Your heart even more. In Jesus' name, amen.

10

{WHY}
Raising Responsible Children Requires Work

It is so much easier to do the laundry myself. It is folded neatly, finished in my time frame and put way exactly the way I like it.

Almost every mother I know claims her clutch on housework over her children because it's easier than training her children to help. Everything always gets done faster and nicer if Mom does it herself.

Mom, I know you work hard. But did you know mothers are naturally inclined to choose easy over hard? Easy means convenience, less strife, and less training. Hard means teaching, training, teaching again. Sometimes the "mean mom" label will be slapped on our backs. I do not want my children to know easy. Sounds gruff, I'm sure. Maybe you want to stick that label on me right now! Don't get me wrong; I would love to give them the easy life. I think we all would love a bit of easy injected into our lives.

But a hardworking child grows into a responsible adult. Don't be afraid to let your children know what hard work looks like. It will grow character and teach them responsibility.

This is where I'm afraid you're going to close the pages of this book, roll your eyes, and think, "All this woman keeps telling me is how much work motherhood is going to be." It is true. Raising responsible children takes work. But the worth of a well-rounded, responsible, hardworking adult is better than turning out a slothful, lazy, grown child.

I choose the worth of work for my family.

Raising Them Up to Grow Beyond Your Hope

Every day I call on God to give me the grace, the perseverance, and a wide view of the future as I train my children to rise to a higher level than even I can teach them.

Dear mama, your ceiling is their floor. You are raising them up toward everything you know and aspire for them to become. Your hopes, dreams, investment, and intentional work become the foundation for their lives. Your reach becomes the platform for their beginnings. Consider the impact of investment: It becomes a greater beginning for your children.

Teaching is not easy. Let's be real. The repeated requests to get a job done, the constant attempts to teach a life skill, dealing with the complaining and whining, and the reminding that helping is not an option and some day they will need to know "these things," may go unrewarded until one day, you will see it. The very worth of your own investment and work.

As we train in diligence, the important question for ourselves and our families is this: How will my actions affect someone else? They need to remember that their actions and attitudes affect other people. If we can keep this question at the forefront of our motherhood and in the lives of our growing children, it will someday be the driving force behind many of their decisions.

Your reach becomes the platform for their beginnings.

If our children were to think about this question every day, imagine the revolution in our culture. This generation does not have to live with laziness or apathy. Teaching your children responsibility will transform your home into a culture void of entitlement.

A home is the foundation of our very essence and the beginning of who we become and where we go. When a family thrives with a heart for service and instills an others-oriented principle, those who enter, live, and leave will thrive in an environment of learning and service.

But when laziness enters the core of a person, a child, or even a community, then the structure will crumble. What is your foundation for training up diligence, hard work, perseverance, and cohesiveness in the heart of your home?

It is our responsibility to raise responsible children.

Where Do You Begin?

Mothers, may I encourage you to not give up, even when your efforts may seem to fall on deaf ears? Remember, every child is different, but when a strong character becomes their foundation you have something to build upon. Discover the possibilities of instilling a good work ethic and don't be afraid to have expectations for change. God expects us to grow to be more like Him, and we want to give our children the opportunities to move outside of their comfort zone. Let's begin together. You've got this!

- **Put away your perfection.** Oh, boy. You like everything done a certain way, and it is going to take effort on your part to be okay with effort over excellence for a time. Our goal is always to bring our children to excellence, but not perfection. When we don't give room for mistakes, differences, or learning, then we hinder our children from learning the value of hard work and effort. This is going to be work for us.

- **Begin with the heart.** Take the time to sit your children down and tell them there will be some changes happening soon, and they are all good. Tell your family that you all be in this together, and start small. Life does not need to be revolutionized in one day. Take small steps in chore training, practicing follow-through, and communicating responsibilities.

- **Show them the way.** Pick an area of training and break the tasks down into small segments. *Show* them, come alongside them, and stick with it—with them. This isn't all about the work, chores, and ability. Remember that life is for service, and you are their example right now.

> ### Truth to Live By
> Whoever fears the LORD has a secure fortress,
> and for their children it will be a refuge.
> The fear of the LORD is a fountain of life, turning a person
> from the snares of death.
> (Proverbs 14:26-27 NIV)

- **Encourage when they show the effort.** Don't be afraid to point out the areas unfinished or not done well. Go back and show your family the areas that were not done completely, and point out how their cutting corners or not being thorough will affect the rest of the family.

- **Ownership is key.** If our children do not own their mess, their roles in the home, their spaces, and their growth, progress, and accountability, then they will never move past a chore chart, nagging instruction, or a checklist they forgot to check. Ownership of any area in life is a huge marker for responsibility. This is the true goal.

- **Take this slowly.** Remember that most of your home can be run by someone other than yourself, if you teach along the way. Your children are the next generation, and although it's hard to see them as adults with adult responsibilities now, keep in mind that the steps you take today will define who they become.

- **Give yourself grace.** *You* are a translator of biblical values. Your words, your time, thoughtfulness, and ability to show compassion, understanding, and "stick-to-itiveness" will show them the way.

How about it? I'd love to sit here with you and tell you this part is going to be easy. But I have learned far more in the work of my motherhood than in the moments of ease and expectancy. This doesn't mean I enjoyed all the tough times of hard work, but I can assure you that there is blessing on the other side of the investment. You are giving your child a lifelong gift of strong character. Integrity is laced into every area of life.

Perhaps you are feeling helpless or hopeless to rally your children to this call. Perhaps your children are set in their ways, or you don't feel you are up to the task. Hear me now, dear friend: You have been given everything you need to do this, including the hearts of your children. Go after their hearts first, work on character, and give yourself grace in this endeavor. Look ahead to the benefits and the transformation possible. And when you feel like you are not getting through to them? Keep working quietly on the small stuff, and they will see your perseverance and diligence. Your ceiling is their floor. Aim high!

Taking the Steps

If you're feeling overwhelmed with what it might take for your child to become responsible, it might be time to take a deep breath and roll up your sleeves. Here are some small steps to take. These probably won't happen overnight and will probably be more for you than your child. I promise every ounce of effort you put in now will reap a lifetime of benefits for everyone. Take time to talk to the Lord and be in the Word before you dive in to raise a more responsible child. It is going to take you *and* God.

Let's Begin Here

1. Identify the areas in your child's life where you would like to see them grow.

2. Ask a friend or family member to point out areas of responsibility where they see your child needs teaching and ownership.

3. Begin listing the jobs, tasks, or details you may be taking care of for your child that they can take responsibility for themselves.

4. Make a plan and work on one new thing a week or month, depending on your child.

5. Ask yourself why you have not started this process before.

   - Was I aware of their lack of responsibility?

   - Was it easier to do those things myself?

   - Do I feel as if my child should not have to help, work, or have accountability as a child?

   - Do I empathize with my child's whining and tears or is it too difficult to deal with their stubborn or lazy behavior?

6. List creative ideas to motivate your child and consequences for a lack of follow-through.

7. Ask yourself: Will I lose heart in this endeavor easily, and should I get someone else on board to keep me accountable throughout the year?

8. Ask yourself: Do I fully realize my child will grow into a selfish adult if I do not work on this area now?

What's Next?

1. Begin teaching your children character that counts. The root of all responsibility is good character and unselfish desires.

2. Make a plan that works for your family. Create charts, checklists, character lessons, accountability plans, and daily chore checks.

3. Remind yourself that it will be easy to give in and allow a privilege to a child who has not shown responsibility.

The hard part is the follow-through and consistent expectations.

4. You will need to train, teach, show, and revisit responsibility in so many areas. Our children will need to see, touch, hear, and be taught what responsibility looks like.

My Parenting Principle

If I want to raise responsible children, I need to be convinced that work and accountability are the best choices for them as they live in my home. I will commit to instructing and following through with age-appropriate tasks and teaching them with patience, love, and consequences. When the teaching and the follow-through are difficult, I need the Lord to help me persevere in prayer and with His promises. I want to raise faithful children.

Dear Lord, this is the toughest place. I am coming to You and asking for fortitude and wisdom when I barely have enough energy to get through my days. Now I feel the heavy weight and realization that I am the one responsible for raising responsible kids. I am downright in need of guidance, and I ask for Your help and Your added measures of grace. I want to raise children who love You supremely and love others well. I know this is part of the process, but I sure could use Your daily presence. In Jesus' name, amen.

11

{WHY}
The Yelling Mom Can Find Hope and Help

A s soon as the words left my mouth I could feel the sting of regret. It was instant. I could see the flash of pain and shock in my child's eyes. Our eyes locked long enough for me to see what I had done. My voice, my tone—they were like a dagger to her heart. It sent her running for her room and left me with the deep cut of regret that I still feel.

That day I met Jesus, face-to-face, outside my daughter's bedroom door as I stood knocking and she refused to answer. I felt defeated and sick to my stomach over my quick reaction to her independent ways. Her questions and her own tone of voice had triggered my frustration, but that was no justification for my actions or reactions. Was I alone in this? No one told me when my babies were born that I may someday yell at them. I wouldn't have dreamed of this day ever happening. My response came from the same heart that loved her more than the world. How could this be?

By the time I had five children ages eight and under, many things had changed. My waistline was shaped a little differently, my schedule was nonstop from dawn to dusk, and I was exhausted. Wrung-out tired, with little to no filter for my thoughts and words. It was beginning to show in my mothering. I didn't have the energy to read a book, search the Word, or ask another woman if this really, truly was "the plan" for motherhood. I asked myself repeatedly if other mothers had such a short fuse. Was this just me? Was I losing control, losing my mind? *Someone, please tell me!* I never once heard another mother in

casual conversation about breastfeeding, diaper wearing, sleep schedules, temper tantrums or teething, ever talk about anger. The anger of
motherhood is the secret kept hidden behind exhausted smiles in the
church nursery and raised grocery lists at the store. Anger and yelling
are the banned responses; the reactions we were sure we would never
allow from ourselves. So when they emerge with force and power on
the days we find ourselves at the end of a short fuse, we're left grasping
and gasping for breath. Alone.

We can't see the whole picture when we are in the middle of it.

But is this an excuse? Couldn't I rein in my tongue when another
mess was made or the children wouldn't listen or pick up their toys on
time? The list of anger triggers began to pile up: Late to church over
another missing shoe, complaints about a dinner that took me too long
to prepare, the child who insists on carving his name onto the bathroom wall with a butter knife, finding the dog food dumped all over
the floor, Legos under the toes in the middle of the night, the whining
over schoolwork. The pushing points became greater than the peace
I had inside.

And so I became the "yelling mom." Not all the time, for I am calm
by nature, but when everything added up, when the pile of "enough"
was to the tipping point, whichever child was in the wrong place at the
wrong time heard the escalation of my voice.

Truth to Live By

When there are many words, transgression is unavoidable, but
he who restrains his lips is wise. The tongue of the righteous is
as choice silver, the heart of the wicked is worth little.
(Proverbs 10:19-20 NASB)

I never yelled a day in my life before I had children. I barely recognized my voice when it came out strong and harsh, and neither did they.
What was happening to me in my motherhood? I didn't like it one bit,
and I know my family didn't either.

Who had I become? I didn't even recognize this person my children knew me to be now.

Hurt Can Lead to Hope

The day of my heart's conviction after the round of yelling at my daughter was significant, painful, and necessary. After getting no response from her side of her bedroom door, I went across the hall to my room. Tears of deep agony were flowing as I sat on the floor with my back against my bed frame. I could hear my daughter's soft cries from across the hall. With my head folded between my knees, I cried loud and hard out to God. I begged Him to take this away, for I knew that He wanted all that was good for me. Sometimes we ask God to take away things that He truly wants us to walk through, even if they are hard. And it is because they are hard that we are being made new.

This part of me was ugly, and it was sin. I knew God didn't want me to be defined by this anymore. The lesson I learned and continue to teach to our children is this: Regret has to equal repentance.

I made my way to my daughter's room with a slow shuffle and long talk with God. He was giving me hope in the midst of a broken heart. I knocked gently, again, on my daughter's door. This time she was ready to hear what I had to say. What I needed to say. After she let me in, I sat on her bedroom floor, facing her with tears still in my eyes and humility in my heart. I could see myself for the imperfect mother I was and still am.

Regret has to equal repentance.

With true childhood grace and love, she mended her heart back to mine. I poured out my remorse, my regret, and my apology for speaking harshly with her. I wish I could tell you that I woke up the next morning a new person. The truth is, God gave me hope that day. He will do the same for every mama.

Are you walking this same path? For every mom who has ever raised her voice, there is hope. Run into the arms of Jesus, and let *Him* transform the very thing you turn over to Him today. And every day.

God Is Your Anchor and Transformation

You may feel as if you are the exception. No one knows your child like you do. Perhaps you're thinking that I never had a strong-willed, independent-thinking child like the one you face daily over the breakfast table. You may feel that your circumstances are harder, or your child is beyond exasperation, or you're just not cut out for this parenting thing.

God gave you the children and the gifts that you have because He wanted you to steward them. He never promised that this would be easy. You may have a unique situation that brings your parenting to challenges and heights that most parents never encounter; but yelling is not the solution. Don't give up. Take heart, dear friend. You are not alone. Learn your limits, give them to God, and identify the points of your frustration even as you work on character training with your children.

You are not alone. And the victory can be yours.

You may be ready to take the steps to stop the yelling and the loss of control over your emotions. Or perhaps you have been convinced you will be the yelling mom forever. I want you to know that your motherhood does not need to be defined by your triggers.

Truth to Live By

Pleasant words are like a honeycomb,
Sweetness to the soul and health to the bones.
(Proverbs 16:24 NKJV)

I know your heart aches and you despise the way anger and frustration change the mom you know you can be. When we barely recognize who we have become, this is the perfect time to let God transform us. Everything in me wants to look you square in the face and tell you that there is good in you, there is a peaceful, quiet mother in there who can face the worst of her motherhood moments and not feel fiery rage coming to the surface. I want to hug you and tell you that you've got

When we
barely recognize
who we have become,

this is the
perfect time
to let God
transform us.

this. But you know what I am going to say. You know it in your heart. *God* is to be your anchor and your transformation. Will you let Him show you?

The quietness and calm is tucked deep in your soul. I know this because we all long for it and recognize it. God settles our feisty spirits with His peace. He allows us to see our children as growing, learning, and sin-filled little people. The anger will go away when we know where it is coming from.

Lean hard into quiet spaces and ask God to transform you from the inside out. Seek to nurture the fruit of the Spirit daily and allow your heart to believe who you are and can be. Friend, we are all walking this path together and holding one another up in prayer and encouragement. There is no judgement here. Motherhood seems to bring out the best and the worst in us. You have a mighty, powerful God who can take your triggers and turn them into beautiful responses. Believe it!

Taking the Steps

There is transformation happening when we are in the pit of pain or discomfort that is the result of our own doing. When we allow God to breathe hope into these times and teach us, we are renewed. Here are some ways you can welcome that transformation with an open heart. I wrote them in the first person so you could own them as your own claims if they suit your spirit's conviction and need, right now.

1. We are all sinners. I should not be surprised when I display my weakness and weariness in this way.

2. God died for this: To give me power, strength, and victory over all through redemption (1 Corinthians 6:14). I need to claim this.

3. Regret will only lead to change through repentance. I should never be too proud to apologize to my children and ask for their forgiveness.

4. I have the power of the written Word. I will memorize

scriptures about the tongue. About the influence of words. About anger and about true love.

5. I will learn to walk away. When I feel the tension in a conversation with my children or a situation that I am completely bewildered by, I will walk away. (This might feel strange, but it can help you to gather your senses and God's peace in the moment.) If I need to leave my kids standing there wondering where I disappeared to for a few minutes, then this is what I'll do.

6. If my child's actions are disrespectful, challenging, or disobedient, and I don't feel that I can handle the situation with the appropriate reaction, then I will ask them to leave the room or I will remove myself from the situation.

7. I will recognize my boundaries, weaknesses, and points of frustration and begin working through those to identify the real reason I am bothered. Is it exhaustion, selfishness, or a lack of training in my children that might be causing the troubling moments?

8. Yelling is not an option. If I work on my heart and the triggers to my frustrations, then my tone and reactions will transform. Identifying my triggers and modifying my responses will require an investment daily.

9. There is no power greater than the Word of God and His authority. With prayer, memorization, and His strength, I can find victory in this area of my life.

10. Little daily changes become big life habits. There is always hope.

My Parenting Principle

My anger does not have to define me. God can remove anger from my reactions, and I can put on a new action. I am willing to humble myself and apologize for anger and ungodly reactions and make a plan to manage my responses better, with practical and godly advice and small steps.

Dear Father, I am tired of hearing my own voice. It is not pleasant at times, and I can understand why my children have stopped listening to me. I need You to help me bring this under control. With surrender, I accept my need for more self-control and give You the rein of my tongue and my words. Lord, please help me to know my triggers and have the strength and clearness of mind in the moments I need to walk away, change my tone, or to tell my children I need to breathe. I want to be able to hear Your voice over mine, and I pray that my children will see how You have given me daily steps in victory, so they will know Your power and might. Thank You for being everything I need. In Jesus' name, amen.

12

{WHY}
You Need to Throw Mom Guilt Out the Window

I will be the first to raise my hand in admission to feeling mom guilt. Sorry for being late, sorry for not picking up the living room, sorry for someone's sadness, sorry for my children's pain. This was me. Sorry for so much, I was practically trying to fix the world and nearly guilted into thinking I could.

There have been times when I realized I was parenting my children out of fear. Fear in motherhood can turn into control. We want to be fixers and menders and make our children happy, but often, we are motivated by guilt, and guilt can look like manipulation. Our attempts to be sorry and fix something, which may not even be ours to fix, heap more weight and burden on our lives than God ever intended for us as mothers.

Guilt and remorse-riddled conversation was my burden for many, many years. Mothers find themselves on a perpetual roller coaster of apologizing and meeting expectations. It's what we do best: Work hard, help our kids, feel like we're not doing enough or doing it perfectly, then apologize. On repeat.

I have beat myself up many times in my years of motherhood. I have made mistakes and held onto fear that I would ruin my children with my inexperience or inability to be a mom. I have rolled out a perfect day for my kids and forgot about myself. I have corrected my children when others thought I was a little too strict and I have made silly rules that I thought were pretty awesome. I have raised my voice when I should have spoken softly; I have been harsh, unpleasant, impatient, and quite frankly, a perfectly ugly mom.

If we chose this to be confessional time, I dare say, you and I could likely list those things we regret as mothers until the sun goes down and comes up again. Yet those things we have learned or wished we could change are to be stepping-stones to growth, not chains about our necks.

Getting Out of God's Way

There is a difference between conviction and guilt. Conviction brings awareness, and when we are aware of those areas we hope to improve or fall short in our motherhood, we work hard to change them. Guilt is owning problems that are not ours to fix. We want our children to be happy, to be the best they can be, and to have everything we think they need. But some things are out of our control.

Guilt is the back-bending, heartbreaking burden you carry around with you every day. It is hindering you from being whole and everything you truly can be for your kids. It will pop up when you least expect it and eventually it will cripple you. No one can carry around guilt and thrive.

This is hard for me to say. I don't like to be preachy, but when it comes to truth, I will give it to you plain and simple: For every little part of your child's life you try to own and fix for them, you are taking away something from the work and worth of God in their lives. Get rid of the guilt over not being enough. He is enough. Get out of God's way.

For every little part of your child's life you try to own and fix for them, you are taking away something from the work and worth of God in their lives.

Oh, I want to be gentle when I say those words. I am the worst guilt hoarder there is. Except I learn to repeat, "Get over yourself." There is no place for guilt when you have God.

I wasted a lot of time and worry thinking that if I just did this and did that, I could create a formula; I could get over the feeling that I wasn't doing enough for my kids. And then, I realized, there *is* a formula for that. But it was created long before I came along.

The gospel.

This is one of the most important life lessons I will share in this book, and I will write it on repeat: The gospel can and will change your children. It will smooth the edges of their entitlement, free you from their debt, and inspire a spirit of gratitude and unconditional love that far surpasses your tireless work to be the hero. It all begins with the gospel. And it puts an end to you carrying the burden of their happiness. Get over it. (The guilt, of course.)

If we made motherhood less about us, what we need to do and need to fix and what may be out of our control, perhaps our children would have more room to grow, bend, and discover that their Creator meets them in all of life's problems and needs. We have somehow equated the role of rearing them with being responsible for their happiness.

Entitlement was not born in the manger, and happiness did not bear its weight on the tree. God never intended for mothers to be the means by which our children succeed, feel superior, or have expectations that place guilt on their lives. Never are we to be bound to the feeling of controlling our children's futures or maneuvering their public life to avoid failure or shame.

What Do They Need?

There is no shame in rest. A common stumbling block for a mother is to feel the need to keep up with the mom next door so her children won't feel deprived, jealous, or in need of anything that might make their world easier or happier. There is no rest in competition, because it will never end. So your children may not be able to take piano lessons or go to dance or art class. They may not have the same snacks the other kids' lunch boxes hold. Or your children may never own the latest and greatest clothes or gadgets. Maybe you didn't enroll them in a sport this year and you served pizza three times this week for dinner because you were running sick children to the doctor and tending to them all through the nights. Your Instagram is not full of creative crafts or cute selfies with your adorable children, and your kiddos' half-hour-a-day screen time is not even close to their friends' allotments. Now you have become the unpopular mom. Sound familiar?

This is how it goes for most women, every day, until the guilt drives them to give in to the "easy" of pleasing the kids and dealing with the consequences later. And we do. From our health to our children's expectations and behavior, every guilt-driven decision we make *for* them will reap a negative consequence down the road. Let me tell you right now: Throw that guilt right out the door and close the door behind you.

Guilt-Free Parenting Means Freedom

Imagine a day when you wake up knowing that your job only consists of loving your children well. That is the only parental responsibility you have today, mama. This sounds so glorious and so unbelievable that I'm sure you are shaking your head in disbelief.

I dare you to try embracing this singular job description today. Feel the freedom in mothering without the guilt driving you to be the most-available taxi driver or the greatest party host. The freedom to say no to your adult children when you just plain need a break. The freedom to tell your family you love them while simply embracing their presence instead of jumping out of your own skin to make life happen for them. The unburdening to say no to a few things and to grasp a new concept of alone time. Loving your children without the compulsion or expectation to fill their happiness tank.

Imagine a day when you wake up knowing that your job only consists of loving your children well.

What Does This Love Look Like

When your children have their character rooted in the gospel, their desires will turn outward. It is like a slow turn of a clock. As they grow more in their understanding of who Christ is and the meaning of the gospel in their lives, the hours turn into days and their choices become less about them and more about others. Raising children to be unselfish can be one of the most unnatural lessons for mothers to learn. Our hearts are inclined to make them happy and to love without boundaries. We mistakenly confuse correction with holding something back from our children. Do not be afraid to call out their selfishness and turn it around. As they grow, their expectations of you will be rooted in true needs and not selfish desires. When this becomes a part of their character, you won't feel such a strong guilt tug-of-war to keep them happy, but rather you will have the deepest desires to do more from your rested spirit because they do not expect it.

Truth to Live By

Let the peace of God rule in your hearts, to which also you were called in one body; and be thankful. Let the word of Christ dwell in you richly in all wisdom, teaching and admonishing one another in psalms and hymns and spiritual songs, singing with grace in your hearts to the Lord. (Colossians 3:15-16 NKJV)

We set our lives up for guilt-driven motherhood from the beginning, but we can work to change this together. I will encourage you, and you can encourage me. After 26 years of parenting, I still want to see my children happy and know that their lives are richly full of abundant grace. And this is my prayer for you today—that you will know the freedom in allowing God to meet your children's needs, and learn to sift through the content of your life that is causing you added measures of stress and guilt.

Often children will realize that their parents would do anything for them and, when moms and dads are weary or tell them no, they learn to use guilt and manipulation to get their desires in the end. It is a fine line for each of us to recognize. Are our actions motivated out of guilt or manipulation or is there something we really need to do?

Taking the Steps

I am going to help you put conviction and guilt into two different categories.

Find a sheet of paper and divide it into two columns. Take a few minutes to write in the first column as many things as you can think of that you do for your family in a day. On the same paper, in the other column, write out the things that you didn't get done, fit in, or wish you could have done for them and still plan to do.

For example, the first column might say this: Helped lay out clothes, bought groceries, took to school, made lunch, cleaned up lunch, picked up their shoes, replaced the toilet paper, swept up the Cheerios, shoveled the sidewalk, buckled them in their car seats, took them to the park, read out loud to them, helped practice piano, reviewed their multiplication tables, made dinner, drove them to soccer, reminded them to bring their water bottles, found their shoes, tied their shoes, found their schoolbooks, and the list goes on.

Include every little detail. Today may look different than yesterday, so take a few days of your life and run them together on your paper. It will be easy to mentally skip over tasks or habits that have become common to you as a mom. Take your time and be sure to include the little things too. Your second list might include a variety of still undone errands and tasks such as: buy school supplies, organize the toy closet, call the sports team moms to plan snack schedules, etc.

Look at your lists. Put a check next to the areas that are focused on happiness for your children. Now circle the areas that are focused on their godliness and growth. Do you see the extra, unnecessary weight and burden you have taken on because of guilt? Sure, there are things we cannot remove from our everyday responsibilities, but we have heaped on more than we need to do and feel the guilt if we do not quite measure up to our own standards. Consider whether the list of things you didn't accomplish is actually a list of important efforts toward godliness and growth or whether they are merely undone tasks that add more guilt and mental stress.

Mom Guilt Comes From:

- Comparison
- Catering to our children
- Disappointment from others
- Getting in the way of God

- Listening to lies
- Others' expectations
- Perfectionism

What Tips Your Guilt Scale Toward Insanity?

What are you doing or owning for your children that they could be doing for themselves?

Make a comprehensive list of the areas of motherhood that usher in stress.

My Parenting Principle

I will learn to manage my time and my energy to give my children what they need and not everything they want. More importantly, I am going to change my own thoughts to knowing that everything I think my children need should be filtered through the lens of God and His desires and provisions for my children. Do my investments have eternal rewards and lasting effects for those around us? Am I helping or hindering?

Wow! Lord, I can see where my imbalance is growing unbalanced children, and I repent of trying to own what should be Your territory for control: my children's lives. They need You, more than they need me, and I have pretty much taken over every area of their lives. Lord, I am asking You to help me raise unselfish children. Will You help me to say no to those areas they can manage on their own? I want to remember that the most important thing I can show them every day is love. Thank You for loving me. I pray that if I give them anything, it will be the gospel. I want holiness more than happiness for my children. Help me, Lord, I pray! In Jesus' name, amen.

13

{WHY}
Interrupting, Whining, and Complaining Don't Have to Control Your Home

A few of the most disruptive and disarming habits children exhibit in their homes are whining, interrupting, and complaining. Combine those three on a daily basis, with multiple children, and even the most patient of mothers will lose her ability to mother well. We don't notice the escalation of our children's behavior until it is out of control. We block out their whining until it unhinges our thoughts and we can't handle the sound anymore. Often we grow a tolerance to these habits, which are rooted in a lack of self-control and selfishness. Everyone has a different tolerance level, but we should be careful to pay attention to where our line has been drawn and ask ourselves this very hard question: "Is any of this behavior ever okay?"

Life Interrupted

Our tolerance to perpetual interrupting can be skirted around with the excuse that we want our children to always feel as though they can speak to us, and we would never want them to feel ignored. Perhaps we have devalued our own work, activities, adult conversations, or quiet space to the point that we'll sacrifice them to allow our children to interrupt us.

Interrupting is rude and selfish. When we make any excuse, other than an emergency, for allowing our children to stop a conversation or to physically pull, tug, or love on us enough that we're distracted from another person's words or eye contact, then we're encouraging and condoning interrupting. The bottom line is this: Your tolerance of this behavior communicates a level of child-centered parenting, and you are teaching your children to devalue others including you.

Have you ever felt guilty about asking your child to wait or for not giving her the attention she thinks she needs right when you are talking with your neighbor or your husband? This is the difference between choosing wisely and being permissive. Your children can learn many valuable lessons from applying a no-interruption rule; it will give them a perspective of respect toward others they may otherwise not have.

The No-Interruption Rule

Before training our children to not interrupt, it's important we have a true conviction to see and value other people and ourselves the way God sees us. When respect is our foundation, our children will be trained in the habit of honoring others.

Truth to Live By

Do everything without grumbling or arguing, so that you may become blameless and pure, "children of God without fault in a warped and crooked generation." Then you will shine among them like stars in the sky as you hold firmly to the word of life. And then I will be able to boast on the day of Christ that I did not run or labor in vain.
(Philippians 2:14-16 NIV)

If we think our children are incapable of waiting for their turn to speak or have attention, it is because we haven't yet realized that we are the ones who created the problem. Ouch, right? Why wouldn't our children expect us to drop what we're doing or stop a conversation midsentence to shower them with focused attention, if this is what we have always allowed? The influence of purposeful parenting comes strongly into play here. You will need to be intentional, committed, and purposeful when you teach your children about honor and respect by breaking the bad habit of interrupting. If this is one of the troubles your family currently faces, are you ready to make a change?

Let's begin with a simple model to help your children visualize what you will be expecting of them in the future. You will let them know that when you are talking or listening to another person, they are not to interrupt with words or by laying their heads on us or leaning hard into our bodies to distract us. Instead, they are to demonstrate a quiet and respectful way of waiting, to show honor to you and to the other person.

It's important to note here that you're not putting your children off or ignoring them, but rather, you're asking them to wait patiently and quietly for a moment by your side. And you will give them a way to communicate with you so they too are honored in this situation. Take your child's hand and gently place it on the side of your hip. Now place your hand over your child's and rest it there. Explain to your child, that when they rest their hand here and your hand covers theirs, they can know that you are aware of their presence and will look for a polite break in the conversation to turn your attention to them. Allow for them to communicate if it is an emergency situation and discuss the difference between an emergency, such as an injury, and a non-emergency, like the strong desire for a snack.

It is important to remind your children that this new way of honoring one another doesn't allow for wiggling, stepping in front of you, tapping you on the arm, or repeating your name until you cannot ignore it any longer. Just a quiet hand on the hip, with your hand resting on theirs, as they take a step to the side.

Mama, they can do this. Can you? It is going to take training at home for a few weeks to get this down. You can try practice times with your family members, with positive words of encouragement and a confirmation to put their mind at ease that you will respond to them soon. It is important to explain *why* they're using the no-interruption rule. Why they honor and show respect toward you and others. Why their needs are not as urgent as they may think, and why you will answer them immediately if it is an emergency. It might take a few times before your children understand what is and isn't an emergency.

This is a life-changing habit that cuts to the core of how we value others and our children. When we remind them of our need for a space that is quiet or sacred and pass along to them a holy view of others, they will use the no-interruption rule with honor and without complaint. This is a great gift you are giving to your child. They will become friends, leaders, coworkers, neighbors, and members of the body of Christ who pay attention to others with a listening mind and heart. The world needs these people now more than ever. It is never too late to begin utilizing this simple habit with your family.

Whining and Complaining

I'm surprised by the amount of whining I hear when I'm in public and how many moms ignore, tolerate, or have given up working on this. Perhaps we have grown accustomed to it in our own homes and don't recognize it in our own children. Or perhaps we excuse it as normal childhood behavior and as something they will outgrow. Behavior is a symptom of the heart. Character will define your children's actions. Give your children a reason to change, and the symptoms will improve. Give them something to change for.

We have never had a child who whined—until recently. Oh, boy! If there is anything you can remember from this chapter, it is this: The habits or symptoms your children have now will only be magnified when they are adults, unless you get to the root of their poor behavior.

Behavior is a symptom of the heart.

Would we recognize whining in our children unless someone pointed it out to us? Whining looks different as our children grow. Whining in a little one or a toddler would be a verbal stream of noise mixed with repetitive requests and demands, and times of hanging on us and crying when they don't get their way. We've all had those times when whimpering and disruptive behavior sabotage a family meal or maybe an entire day. This can come in small doses or large verbal fits that everyone can hear. Mothers often give in to these symptoms because of their inability to get it to stop. It can feel insurmountable at the time, can't it? Which is exactly the purpose of whining in the first place. Whining is a behavioral effort to control an environment. Ultimately, it is a pure demonstration of a lack of self-control. And just like the habit of interrupting, this behavior comes from a me-first perspective.

In our preteen children, we will notice whining in a new form. You may notice sullenness when they don't get their way, or repetitive questions about the same thing, asked differently each time, with the sole purpose of wearing us down. Their voice may be angry or upset, and we may hear words like, "It isn't fair," or "This doesn't make any sense." Often their whining evolves into complaining and it becomes so grating, we will give in out of guilt or seeking relief from the nagging.

We all whine, don't we? Babies, tweens, teens, and adults. It's our selfish desires coming out strong. Rather than being upset with our children about their behavior, we can be sympathetic in trying to understand how important their circumstances are so we can understand their behavior in context and respond appropriately.

Mama, you would be surprised how early you can teach your children good communication skills. Whining does not have to interrupt your day and cause big meltdowns or bring a halt to your activities. The secret is to do your training at home. I have witnessed complete meltdowns of children *and* their mothers in public, some attempting to parent in the moment, for the whole world to see, and with little success. Whining is a symptom of the behavior you'll need to identify and correct at home.

> Give your children a reason to change, and the symptoms will improve. Give them something to change for.

Whining Be Gone

I want you to read this with an underlying hope, during the hard moments, of nipping this whining thing in the bud. Your heart will need to be assured that it is okay to tell your children "no more" to whining. But you'll consistently need to remind yourself that if you continue to allow the negative behavior, the little person whining in front of you will eventually be a bigger person with a bigger attitude and a louder voice.

Begin with their demands and remind yourself to consider if they are about something your child needs or wants. Once you have distinguished this, you can point out their tone and their insisting demands of repetition and ask them to stop. Remind your children, "We do not whine; we ask." When and if the whining continues, use a warning and ask them if they can hear their voice and tell them it does not sound nice and no one wants to listen to their noise. Give them an example of a nice voice, a nice way of asking, and require that they try this with you. Once they have noticed your joy and their peace over the change in their behavior, the whining becomes less and less of a predominant factor in their lives. It will take time and fortitude. We can be loving and sweet, yet unmoving in our intolerance of the whining and complaining. Tell your child you would love to listen but you cannot hear them when they ask, demand, or speak that way. Remind them to only ask one time in a nice voice and you will be happy to answer them.

Sounds too easy? Better read than said? I can honestly share that the biggest obstacle in a mother's attempt to curb the whining in her children is most often the mother herself. Often we doubt children's ability to comprehend and we tolerate poor behavior until the teaching moments have passed. It may take some time for you and your child to work this out together. The responsibility to change falls on your shoulders, as much as it does theirs. Do not doubt the age and ability of your child. Young babies are able to learn to not whine, as are teens who have turned their whining into manipulation. Age is not a barrier to a change of heart and bad habits being transformed. We all just need an example, a good motive, and follow-through.

Truth to Live By

Let no corrupting talk come out of your mouths, but only such as is good for building up, as fits the occasion, that it may give grace to those who hear.
(Ephesians 4:29 ESV)

Model What Matters

I have met families with more than they could ever ask for, and yet the comments that came from the mouths of the parents were negative and critical. Their children knew nothing different and had the same language and attitude. Our culture today is about self-gratification, and we may make excuses for our children when we feel they "deserved something," or something "wasn't fair." This mental state while raising children will reap discontented adults and a whole new generation of discontented families.

If we don't want our children to be complainers, then we must examine our view on those gifts that God has truly given us and learn to temper our tongues. Complaining is rooted in ungrateful spirits and negativity. This can be born out of our parenting process and the culture of our homes. Perhaps it's time to do a little housecleaning and find the positive and edifying words that may be missing from our lips and a grateful spirit in our hearts.

Taking the Steps

Motherhood is hard enough. Then add in a lot of extra and unnecessary noise on top of the workload? It seems we would be desperate to eliminate those things that we could fix.

Some things take years of investment and work to see a harvest, and then there are those things like interrupting, whining, and complaining, which can see almost immediate results.

Start today by teaching your children how to calmly come alongside you and make their presence known by placing their hand at your hip and awaiting your hand to be placed atop their own. The more you practice this with them, the more confident they will feel to do this when you are speaking to others out in public or at home.

To help your family discover new ways of communicating that don't involve whining and complaining, create a list of words and phrases that build up and a list of those that tear down. When the language in the house is becoming negative, remind everyone of the positive words. Make it a fun household challenge to use only the uplifting words. Every great habit starts with practice!

My Parenting Principle

If I hope for my child's external behavior to have symptoms of unselfishness, gratefulness, and contentment, I must give them daily examples of this and help them put off poor behavior and put on positive, godly behavior. It's not impossible to train my children to put off whining, complaining, and interrupting, but I must see the symptoms before I can address it. Acknowledgment is the first step to positive change. Excuses give reason for selfishness and stunt growth. My children will only grow as far as I lead them.

Lord, I am tired of the whining and complaining. It is wearing me down, and I want to give up on trying. I'm at a loss. I know I need Your help in this more than anything. You reached my heart. Will You help me reach theirs? Will You give me the endurance to guide them toward positive behavior and allow their lives to be molded more into an image of You? In Jesus' name, amen.

14

{WHY}
Most of Our Motherhood Will Be Spent on Our Knees

Your everyday mundane is your child's lifeline. Your love for your children propels you to do the small things, the big things, and every little thing that goes unnoticed. We are the very example of love, sacrifice, mercy, and hard work that they will see as they grow. Motherhood does not have a pay scale worthy of its work, but our example is not going unnoticed. Our children are watching. They see our deliberate choices and actions. They watch us work with our hands and hustle and bustle until our bodies cannot give one more ounce of love. Yet our most potent and powerful sacrifice of love, which our children rarely see, is our time spent in prayer. The sanctification of motherhood is in the bowing low when we have no control, no ability to change their hearts, their circumstances, or their actions.

Truth to Live By

The Holy Spirit helps us in our weakness. For example, we don't know what God wants us to pray for. But the Holy Spirit prays for us with groanings that cannot be expressed in words.
(Romans 8:26 NLT)

When a hardened heart gets in our way, there is always God. God wants us to remember that our children are on loan. They are His. And we need Him to give us the courage and the humility to come to Him on their behalf.

The Power of Your Example

"He slapped me across the face." We will never forget these words from one of our sons. He arrived home from an event where one of his leaders took his anger and frustration out on our son. Compelled to react with a force to be reckoned with and make matters right, we needed to remember that our son was watching us. The restraint it took for us to hold back an unrighteous response took great self-control and effort. We followed the story to the root of the problem and pursued it to the end. The builder felt indignation and frustration at the example another adult had set for our son, and the injury to his boy's heart and pride. After our own deliberation and a conflict-free confrontation, our son received an apology. We worked through the effects this had on our son for years. This was not heroic. It was our job—our responsibility to make this right and to seek justice. We poured out hours of prayer with our son during hours of sleepless nights over the hurt and the pain our son would have to work through. Prayers are the most powerful words of all.

God wants us to remember that our children are on loan. They are His.

Every parent knows the sleepless nights, the giving and the taking, and the praying moments that bring us to our knees, when we beg God to intervene or give us wisdom for things we cannot know. Receiving late-night calls, driving to meet your child after a car accident, watching them hospitalized for illness for weeks on end, battling the influence of the world that can seep through the cracks of your home, and standing in the gap when they are too weak to put on their own armor: This is the everyday knee-bending work that our children will never see.

Your children won't ever understand the labor involved in letting the chips fall where they may when everything in you calls to rescue them from their own mistakes and circumstances. They won't witness all the times you call out to God for the spiritual discernment it takes to battle for their hearts.

All of this—every waking, crying minute—will happen on your knees in prayer.

There is no greater sacrifice you can make for your children in this world than to pray over their lives every single day.

The true badge of courage will be a crown in heaven—a reward for the faithful who knew during their lifetime that any heroic act our children see us do is covered in prayer and given to God. This is love. It's unconditional, unwavering love that cannot be taken away because we are tired, weary, or over-the-top tired of the same old excuses. This heroic love will not end when their decisions tax our pocketbooks or our patience. It is unseen and unrewarded until the moment we take our last breath, because the love we have for our children is woven into our prayers and the whispers we give to God, even when it's time to say good-bye.

We Cannot Fix Everything

Mothers are fixers. We are called to do and fix everything when our children are babies and, then out of the blue, we need to discern when and what we should fix for them. We have to hold back that first impulse to make everything better. It is a tug-of-war of a mother's heart. Fix it or leave it. Step in or step aside. No one could ever tell you which is the right answer in every situation. This is where prayer and supplication to the Lord is vital.

Calling on the name of the Lord gives us the freedom to cry out in anger, fear, and frustration for wisdom in raising the children He gave us. Our job is too important to trust our own decisions alone, especially when we are in the thick of emotional moments.

Truth to Live By
Pray in the Spirit at all times and on every occasion. Stay alert and be persistent in your prayers for all believers everywhere. (Ephesians 6:18 NLT)

Yes, motherhood is heroic. But we all know that heroes stumble because of their own weaknesses. Motherhood cannot be done alone. We need God, His Word, His promises, and the time to include Him into our spaces, where the foundation and the unnoticed work really gets done. Motherhood matters to God. He would never give us a gift and leave us wondering what to do with it. He desires for us to include Him, to trust His plan, and to show our children that we could never do this without Him. That's the secret to being the best mom.

Your children will someday know the sacrifice of your labor in love, and not because of how weary you may become or how much you tell them you did for them; they will know that you bent your knee, pleaded on their behalf, and that God intervened when you were too weak to do more. This is the true badge of courage. To give credit where credit is due. To know that when we are weak, God is strong—and to give God the glory so that our children will rise to call us blessed and call on the name of the Lord (Proverbs 31:28).

Taking the Steps

Your most worthy moments in motherhood will be on your knees. There is no lower place than bowing low and giving God your motherhood on the altar as a sacrifice. Our hidden investment is our most trusted work. How can we be at peace with our kids' choices, cry in quiet over their pain, and wait for their listening hearts to find their way?

- **We pray without ceasing.** In the long hours of the night, when they walk out the door and when they sit and pour out their hearts to us, we pray. We call on the name of the Lord for direction, intercession, and wisdom. We ask for peace and for help, and we give them back to God.

- **We cry out with our pleas, anger, and our confusion with humility.** God doesn't expect us to have the answers. He is waiting for us to call on His name and ask. He gives wisdom freely when we ask, and His strength is always available to us when we lean on Him. Our children need our intercession on their behalf.

- **We give God control.** Maneuvering and controlling our kids in our own power to keep them in tune with God will never reap a genuine heart connection between our children and the Lord. God wants all of us and all of our children.

- **We tell God our woes.** When we feel ashamed at our mistakes and are afraid we have messed up, we need to confess, to ask God to forgive us and lead us in a way of repentance to our children. The strongest words a parent can ever use to lead their children by example are "I'm sorry." Humility grows honesty, love, forgiveness, and respect. God provides all of those for us. Motherhood is an honor.

- **We talk to God rather than preach at our kids.** Tell Him what confuses you about your child's behavior or choices, and ask God what to do about it. Wait for His answer. Put away your preaching, and replace it with listening for God's leading.

My Parenting Principle

When I remember the Giver of the gifts I have been given, I will return to Him for guidance. God did not expect me to have all the answers for motherhood. I will commit to giving my worry, my concerns, and my fears to God. I will lay my motherhood on the altar of thanksgiving and prayer, expectantly listening for His provision. My children need God more than my opinions and fear-filled concerns. When I feel defeated, I will stand tall in the power of His might. When I see my children failing, I will pray for their lives to be upright and full of God's wisdom. When I fear their danger or fall prey to anger over their decisions or actions, I will call on the name of the Lord and ask for His strength and peace.

Father, I commit my children to You. I have taken on the whole burden of leading and loving, and it is too heavy to carry anymore. Will You help me to daily give this over in prayer to You? I hand the lives You've entrusted to me back to You for the wisdom and direction we need. I am guilty of feeling the weight of those things I cannot control. Will You walk with my children when I am not present? Will You take them by the heart and the hand and lead them where I cannot? Motherhood has me all tangled up in a knot of love, and I want to give my children what they need, but I know You can give them so much more. I give my motherhood to You. Not just bits and pieces or my leftovers, but all of it. In my quiet places, I seek You today. In Jesus' name, amen.

Let's Talk

I feel as if we should have a pause button right here. I am envisioning you with your hand poised to turn the page, but your heart is still beating fast from everything you feel you need to work on and your mind is reeling from taking so much in. If this describes you, I want to throw you a rope of hope. I am compelled to give you a shot of inspiration and encouragement.

Your motherhood is influential. No one else can do your job like you can. God handpicked you to be the mother of your children, and He will provide you every tiny thing you need. If there is any reason to keep going, to keep reading, or to keep on in your motherhood, it is that you are valued and loved beyond compare.

I want to come sit beside you as we venture into the next chapters together. With my arm around your back and my head nodding to you in affirmation, I say to you, *you can do this*. You can finish strong what God began, even if you feel zero strength, creativity, or fortitude to carry on. When you turn this page, you will find fresh ideas to give your children the motivation to learn and grow with you and not against you.

If there were one thing I could say to you face-to-face right now that has made the biggest impact on my motherhood, it would be this: Be honest and humble with your children. Respect and honor are never born in lies and pride. Many moms shake their heads wondering why their children don't come to them with

> God handpicked you to be the mother of your children, and He will provide every tiny thing you need.

mistakes or weakness. We wonder what to do when we have blundered our way through messy moments and when we don't have the answer to all their whys. The solution: We tell them we are a work in progress.

Motherhood is a legacy of love, and our children can learn from our open and honest communication. This is us right here and now. Give me your hand and I will walk with you. This is your invitation to purposeful parenting. I want to encourage you to finish strong so your legacy will not be left unfinished.

Part III

{WHY}
You Will Lead Them in the Way They Should Go

*Now you are deep in what seems to me a peculiarly
selfless service. The spiritual training of children
must be that. You work for the years you will not
see. You work for the Invisible all the time, but you
work for the Eternal. So it is all worthwhile.*

AMY CARMICHAEL

15

{WHY}
Raising Children with Faith Will Mean More Than Anything You Can Teach Them

The groove of motherhood had settled in my bones, and the routine required by our family of five finally seemed to be synchronized. It had been a strong learning curve, from our firstborn son to baby number three, but the routine of my role as a mama finally felt normal and not quite so suffocating. I was far from thriving, but I knew I had been learning, and the daily practice of applying new things to our lives seemed to be bringing my purpose into perspective. It seemed so complicated and busy while I was living those earlier years, but now I look back on that part of my personal journey and miss the smallness of my world. It was a time of simplicity, innocence, and amazement as my husband and I learned everything together.

God gave us so much grace in those years as we maneuvered through the routine, the sleep deprivation, the illnesses, our health journeys, our rented homes, our personalities, and our love. While I was learning to be a mother, the kids were taking in the fullness of the love life we lived. There were so many lonely, long hours to fill that I had to be more creative than ever before. We spent hours reading, singing, walking, talking, and learning, all the while growing as a team. When my creative ideas ran out, and those three kiddos relied on me to figure out the very next step, I ran to God. I quickly realized that my care and creativity wasn't enough. I could only teach, love, give, and give some more; and then I would find myself on empty.

I needed God, and so did my children. He became an integral

part of our conversations, our walks, our reading, our singing, and our learning. I began to weave Him into my mothering, and His presence became intertwined with our daily lives. My motherhood was not my own, and I quickly realized that my children needed more than knowledge or amazing childhood memories to fall back on. They needed Jesus more than they needed me or anything else for that matter.

Life was good. God was good.

Faith in the Darkness

And then a testing like no other rocked our foundation, and everything I knew and loved dearly became more important to me. We were expecting twin baby boys when I started to experience complications and received a troubling prognosis. A daily waiting game seemed to bring our happy, comfortable life to a screeching halt. Dear God, I felt forsaken and forlorn.

Physical pain can creep into your bones and unsettle your outlook on life. It can change you. It is unfathomable to me, in my worst moments, to imagine the clarity of thought and purpose that Jesus had on the cross in His last moments of suffering. He never wavered from His divine purpose to bring our pain and brokenness upon Himself and to bear it for our future. He lived every breath until the end for us.

Pain shatters lives, and it was beginning to break me apart in places I didn't know existed. It shook my faith. It shook the very fiber holding our happy family together. My motherhood was tightly bound up in faith, but now it was unraveling quickly.

You give any woman a deadline or a projected date to receive an outcome and she will run strong to that finish line. If she knows it, sees it, or can focus on the destination, she will always give it her all. Twenty-five weeks' gestation was the goal for our twin baby boys, and I was in for the long haul. Three times a week, the doctor performed an amniocentesis, drawing large amounts of extra fluid from my womb. The doctor maneuvered his needle around our growing babies who were tightly packed into their mama's belly. Active and identical, the babies shared the same blood supply and were as close to my heart as they were one another.

During each procedure, we could watch our boys on the ultrasound screen. My heart was knit closer and closer to them as we said hello to their beautiful faces a few times a week and watched them grow in my womb. What an amazing window into their tiny lives. It revealed glimpses of them holding hands, leaning against one another, and breathing steady breaths together. They were beautiful. Luke and Aaron—two more boys. This would make four boys and one girl when they were born. My husband was ecstatic, and I was pushing through the pain and waiting for the finish line. Twenty-four weeks and counting.

Live Your Faith, So They May Believe

Every day in my new normal meant physical limitations for my motherhood. It meant the inability to invest in everything I had been pouring my heart into for the last five years. I began to ask God for my faith to be on my terms, as I watched my little ones with new eyes. Eyes of a mama who knew her own life was in danger and wondering if this is all really worth it. How much can a heart take? It didn't seem fair that I had been pouring out my life daily and now I might be told to give every bit of that up. But what had I been teaching my children?

Truth to Live By

I pray that you, being rooted and established in love, may have power, together with all the Lord's holy people, to grasp how wide and long and high and deep is the love of Christ, and to know this love that surpasses knowledge—that you may be filled to the measure of all the fullness of God.
(Ephesians 3:17-19 NIV)

When you face the core truth of every little thing that held you together, that moment becomes the why of what you have been living and teaching. When this happened to me, I had to trust God even though I felt so out of sync with the life around me. I watched friends and family come and go, caring for my children and our home. I spent hours cuddling and resting with my little ones from my second-story apartment bedroom. The rest of their active days and happy giggles were spent out of my sight as I had to conserve energy and make trips to the doctor's office for more procedures. I felt the loss of control and management of my home and my motherhood. Would anything ever feel normal again?

Faith Is Believing

Surrender.

In complete surrender, I fell to my knees, by my son's crib, crying out to Jesus to have His will, knowing my heart would have to follow. He was waiting right there for me to give the control back to Him. For months, my children had watched this painful process that was sucking the life right out of me. The beautiful thing about motherhood? Your investment plants deep roots that cannot be wiped out by trial and hardship. My little ones seemed quite unfazed by the upheaval in their schedules and the change in my attention to their everyday lives. Everything we had set in motion in their lives seemed to continue as before. I watched them thrive even when I felt I was failing them. I could see them cling to my responses and wait for my smiles. In the simplest of ways, they unknowingly met my needs when my faith was small and my body was weak. They were trusting me as they always had. I was the one wavering, and they waited. And watched. What would happen? Would they believe when my faith was weak?

The beautiful thing about motherhood? Your investment plants deep roots that cannot be wiped out by trial and hardship.

Their eyes searched mine when I cried. When we went for short walks by the creek side, I could see their little minds working through the struggle of wondering why mommy was sad. We would talk about tadpoles and look under rocks. I would take more time than ever before searching the deep pools of reflection as they peppered me with questions about God: How He made water, how He made the sun. And always, always they would ask about their baby brothers. My children began to minister to me in their childlike faith. Asking questions that I had begun to ask myself. The simplest and most foundational truths that I believed, but that now wavered from moment to moment when I allowed fear to crowd out my trust and I asked why. Their joy, their songs, the verses we had worked on together as a family ministered to me. From the faith deeply rooted in their lives, I was being blessed.

Faith always shines brighter than darkness. The little light we had been growing in their tiny minds and lives over the years would shine through the cracks of my polished and brave exterior. It always does. Light is drawn to light.

This Little Light of Mine

The day that the Lord set my first child's heart on fire was the day that I turned over the earth onto a small white casket and said goodbye to our twin boys. The drive home was dark, and my heart had lost the will to give, to invest, and to just keep pressing on. We had made it to 24 and a half weeks with our baby boys. *So close*, was all I continued to repeat in my heart. So close to the finish line. Except Luke and Aaron had finished so beautifully and were with our heavenly Father. I was completely and utterly wrecked, broken, and holding onto hope with the finest strand of strength left in me. Motherhood is a capture-and-release process set on repeat. I just wished I had more to hold on to after the pain washed away.

But we know God is working even when we cannot see; and when we have lost all hope, He shows His mighty power and redemption. He showed me the future that dark day and reminded me that everything has a purpose. Even when we cannot see it.

It jolted me. The question from our son, rising above the backseat and into our ears.

"Are my baby brothers with Jesus?"

Be still my heart.

"Yes. Yes, they are."

His voice was confident and sure. "I want to be with Jesus when I die. Will I go there too?"

It had been one hour since I said good-bye to a piece of my motherhood, and my oldest was asking to give *his* life to Jesus. That night, I saw the future. I saw past the darkness and realized that every moment matters to God. And I was not going to lose another moment of investment in the future.

This day turned the page on my son's future and mine. It gave me vision and a spark to ignite a passion in my children that will change the world and bring hope and light to the dark places.

If God could turn death into life for one child, and use me to help, then I wanted more of this passion and pursuit.

Taking the Steps

When we identify our pursuits, we realize our passions. If living a life of faith has not become a part of your routine or habits, this is the time to make some changes. We do not always feel an urgency to make any drastic changes when it comes to living out our faith. Is it merely enough for our kids to know there is a God and allow them to find their own way? This idea is convenient, until you are face-to-face with man's depravity and the hardship of this world and the fact that without Jesus, we all walk a path that will lead to death. Where will we direct our kids when this time comes?

Let's consider the seriousness of making our faith so real to our children, it becomes their lifeline. Mothers worry: what will they do when something comes into their lives (and many things will) that will take them away from teaching their children or being there for them? God fills in the gaps. He does. But we want our kids to know *who* He is before that inevitable day arrives.

My Parenting Principle

I realize I cannot be everything my children need. Unless I give them a daily dose of the living, breathing God in their life, when the day comes that I cannot be there or fix something, they won't know to rely on God first. Even before me. I am going to pray over my children's lives for a deep faith that is rooted in places I cannot reach, and that my faith will be strong enough to know He is enough for my children.

Father, I come to You with a heart desiring wisdom and strength to lead my children to You. Will You grant me the wisdom and direction to show them what faith is? I want to teach them so much, Lord. I realize You are in everything. Father, You are my lifeline, and I pray that I will reach the hearts of my children with Your love. I pray that they will someday make You their own and serve You with a glad and committed heart. Help me, Lord. I pray in Jesus' name, amen.

16

{WHY}
A Mother in the Word Can Lead Her Family Well

I have spent hours reading books on motherhood, and I have read many blogs on the best way for moms to be in the Word. When women find a personal key to success, they are eager to share it with everyone. And there are a lot of stories and testimonials out there. For this I am thankful, but may I throw out the bottom-line truth? There is only one way to lead your family well. It is to be in the Word and know your purpose.

Here's the reality we need to check in with every day: Your motherhood and the use of your time need to fit your personal life. The joy a woman feels when she has created a schedule, a balance, and a purpose for her family is monumental.

And the flipside can be true as well. You can become grumpy, sad, or resentful over your lack of time or inability to get into God's truths, but this is not the light we hope to shine for our family and friends while pursuing Jesus. Right? Go easy on yourself. No one wants a miserable mother who blames her surroundings, her children, and her busy life as the very reason she is not in the Word. So, what's a mom to do?

Put Off to Put On

Every day I remind myself that being in the Word will grow a desire in me to change and to grow. The daily practice of removing the bad habits and putting on the habits from the Word enables me to lead my family well. When the Word convicts me in those areas where I need to change, the biblical principle of putting off the old and putting on the new becomes my next step.

As busy mothers, we might be prone to wandering when distractions arise. The struggle is real. I don't know if there has been any habit harder to form since I have become a mother than making the time to be in the Word.

If you are like me, when free time arises, you are inclined to either sit and close your eyes for a few minutes of quiet or complete a task from start to finish for the first time in forever. When it's difficult to carve out time for the basics, how in the world can a mom find moments for meaningful time in the Word?

I have discovered that when I am at my lowest, weakest point, the time I have invested in the Word provides a return that never runs dry. The truth and comfort I have drawn from my times of reading, studying, and being present with the Lord seem to be readily available when my other crutches of strength or self-reliance are gone.

Truth to Live By

Commit yourselves wholeheartedly to these words of mine. Tie them to your hands and wear them on your forehead as reminders.

(Deuteronomy 11:18 NLT)

We need to ask to drink from springs of living water on a regular basis if we want to draw from God's supply when life depletes us (John 4:10). And we all know that is inevitable. I have discovered that the one constant and steady habit that keeps me full of hope and sustains me in my hardest, loneliest, most broken times is my time with God. Reading God's Word gives life because He is the living Word. He is the well that will never run dry.

We don't have enough wisdom, fortitude, patience, or endurance to raise children without God's sovereign grace and knowledge. I would be a fool to think I could do this without the Lord. Every day I search Scripture for an answer, a prayer, a verse of encouragement, or His direction in raising my children. It is my desire to be the best mom I can be for my children; but I know that when I'm coming up short because of my inability to stay in tune with Jesus, then my motherhood and their lives come up short as well.

The Struggle Is Real

There is so much value in seeking wisdom from others who have found rest in their routine and refreshment in His Word. Yet we sometimes run the risk of putting these women on the Super-Christian Women pedestal and go to them for help, advice, and tools when we could go to directly to God and His Word for our help. Simply put: At a certain point your relationship with God and His Word has to be formed between you and Him. May I strongly urge you to remember a few life-changing principles?

1. The struggle to be consistent remains with us all. We can seek encouragement to try new things, but when it comes down to the grit of it, it will be you and God.

2. Seeking advice and gleaning wisdom has value, but our motivation should be rooted in our daily need for His life-giving words. If you find your motivation lacking, consider your children. Motherhood should be one of the single most driving motivators for you to seek His face more every day. Our children need us to need Him.

3. The Word of God will trump new ideas, plans, and any "best kept secrets" a human leader can share. Open the pages to your Bible and find how His truths are real and relevant to your everyday messy and glorious motherhood. He is all you need. Even more than that coffee. The struggle is real. I get it.

Everyday Moments of Truth

There are so many moments in my motherhood when I literally speak out loud to God and tell Him I have no idea what I am doing. It sounds crazy, considering that I'm writing a book on motherhood. But the real, bottom-line truth is this: You cannot do motherhood alone.

Motherhood and Jesus are a package deal. Don't try one without the other. You'll be cheating your kids and yourself out of something amazing! He is your lifeline!

The two top hurdles keeping women from finding their way to the Word are *desire* and *time*. In order to pursue time in the Word, we must put something else off. Comb through your schedule to see what can go, be moved around, or changed to give you some sacred time.

Finding this space is the first step. After that, where do we begin, and what will this look like for each of us? It will be different for you, so be sure to cut out the comparing right off the bat. When my children were little, my time to be in the Word was the evenings, with a plan to read a little in the Old Testament, a little in the New Testament, a small part of Proverbs, and a small portion of Psalms. I began to memorize Scripture for the first time in my life and it was one of the most difficult things I have done mentally as an adult. I was astonished. But once your mind is in a regular practice of memorizing, it becomes easier and more rewarding.

You are a vessel to hold His Word, and its wisdom will pour into your motherhood when needed. Don't be discouraged with the struggle to stay focused while reading or any inability to understand or see the big picture of the Bible when you begin reading His Word. We often have lofty expectations when we meet with God, and we should. But, He is the One who will give you what you need. It is our humanity, our exhaustion, and our distracted hearts and minds that often get in the way. Anything worth pursuing will take time and perseverance. Don't give up. What's the most rewarding thing about reading, memorizing, resting in the Bible and in the presence of God? It never leaves you. Go after it with great anticipation, and your motherhood will be transformed.

You will have times in the desert. Moments when you feel far away from God's heart or the practice of seeking His heart. Are you surprised I would say this? It's the truth. I want you to know this and be prepared

You cannot do motherhood alone. Motherhood and Jesus are a package deal.

for your plan to fall apart. Why? We are moms. Our days are teetering on the delicate balance that everything will go as planned and we will have no major interruptions or catastrophes. It's inevitable that we will stray from the plan, the path, the perfect day. When this happens, we need to give ourselves grace. God wants us to seek Him when we are thirsty. Just keep coming back to the well and draw your strength and wisdom from Him.

Taking the Steps

Let's begin together, right now, right here. Will you take five minutes to read through a few of the verses I'm about to share here with you? Why not begin together? I have read, reread, and applied these scriptures to my motherhood for many years. What a wonderful place to begin—right where God can meet you every day in the life that you have chosen to make matter. He is the Great Provider and Sustainer, so let Him use these verses to be an encouragement to you as you begin to see the value of just five minutes in His truths. Let your time expand with your heart. Remember, your time seeking God will forever change the future of your motherhood.

Topic	Scripture
My Choices:	Psalm 1
My Spiritual Growth Exam:	Psalm 4
Focus on the Future:	Psalm 16
Prayer and Praise:	Psalm 27:14, Psalm 28:7, Psalm 31:7, Psalm 100
Desire for God:	Psalm 42
Help and Comfort:	Psalm 46
Pour Out Your Heart:	Psalm 62
Prayers for Our Children:	Psalm 78
Knowing Christ During Crisis:	Psalm 86

146 * Why Motherhood Matters

God's Love and Our Response:	Psalm 103
My Christian Walk:	Matthew 5
Everyday Faith:	Hebrews 11
Living Out My Faith:	James
My Tongue:	James 3
My Walk with God:	1 Peter
Seek His Face:	Psalm 105:4-5
Real Peace in His Presence:	Psalm 139
Seeking True Wisdom:	Proverbs
Call to Action:	Proverbs 4
Sowing Humility and Righteousness:	Proverbs 10–11
Yielding Fruit:	Proverbs 12
Tongue of the Wise Woman:	Proverbs 13–14
Soft Answers:	Proverbs 15:1
Committing Our Work and Wisdom to God:	Proverbs 16
Our Words:	Proverbs 16:24-25
Considering My Actions:	Matthew 7
Judging:	Matthew 18
Forgiveness:	Matthew 18
My Responsibility:	Matthew 22:37-40
My Calling:	Luke 3:4-6
While We Work for God:	Romans 8
Practical Christian Living:	Romans 12
Edification:	Romans 15
Joy and Thankfulness:	Philippians
Perseverance:	2 Corinthians 4

My Salvation in Action:	Ephesians 2
Communication:	Ephesians 4
Armor of God for the Everyday Battle:	Ephesians 6
Contentment:	Philippians 4
Rejoicing in the Lord:	Philippians 4
Motherhood:	Colossians 3
Faithfulness:	1 Thessalonians 5
Memory Work:	John 1, Romans 12, James 1, Matthew 5, Psalm 1

My Parenting Principle

If my motherhood is going to matter, then I need to drink from springs of living water. I will begin to pray for a daily desire and the grace to get in God's Word before anything else. God can transform my life from the inside out, and my children need to see Him glorified in my surrender and my time with Him.

I need more time with You, God. Right now, I pray that my heart and mind will yearn for You. Will You grant me a strong desire to give You my best? I know You are the vital lifeline I need to get me through and help me thrive in the places where I have no hope. Help me, Jesus. Open my eyes as I read the pages of Your Word, and allow me to retain the truths so I can teach my children. You are my one and only God. Thank You for meeting me right here where I am. I give this day, this need, and my heart to You, God. In Jesus' name, amen.

17

{WHY}
Family Devotions Matter
(and Whose Job Is It Anyway?)

For many years I carried an attitude of sadness, disappointment, and confusion over how we spent time in the Word of God as a family. I begged the Lord to help my husband get on board and to lead us well, but the whole time I prayed, it was as if I had this large beam in my eye and couldn't see past what I called his "shortcomings." If I'm honest with myself, I would say I thought I was marrying a strong spiritual leader. Perhaps it was because he was raised in a pastor's home, or perhaps because our relationship was forged over the Word. I felt deceived. Through every experience of birthing, growing, schooling, and nurturing our babies, I craved the Word and biblical leadership in our home.

I was not raised in the Word. As a kid, I knew of the Bible. I held it in my hands, and I was even encouraged to read and study it; but never had I lived through it. I was a mother raising the next generation now, and my primary focus (other than sleep) was to weave the Word into our family DNA.

My desire for my man to lead us in the Word had become an idol. I had placed it so high on my list of expectations that I began to grow discontent in my heart. It is easy to lose sight of the good intention behind a desire when it becomes distorted into a demand. I had become the woman who held the Word as an idol of perfection over the headship of my husband, and it began to cause a mountain of unnecessary stress to all of us.

I begged him to lead us in the Word at night. He would sit at the head of our table and open the Bible. As he quietly turned to a section he had chosen to read and share, I would find myself annoyed by the job of keeping the children quiet while he read and spoke to them. I would ask him to read louder or with more animation, to keep their interest. I suggested he might read this, or say that. I even corrected my builder when his quiet reading might have been too "boring" to the kids. Of course, I thought I was being discrete and helpful with the family's best interest in mind. But really it was my pride poking through with selfish desires, and it reeked rancid compared to the Word I was asking the builder to read in our home. I was all wrapped up in what should be, rather than what could be.

When Our Desires Turn to Control

When women attempt to mold or model their husbands into an idol set up in their minds, then idols will do what idols do: Come crashing down. This is exactly what happened in the heart of our home. My good intentions and desires had been taken over by my emotional response. The very heart of the one thing I wanted supreme, to be in the Word as a family, was tarnished by my control.

Perhaps the Christian culture has painted a perfect, unachievable model of family leadership, devotions, and how our personal time in the Word should look, and we have been led to think that every family is to look the same. Often we confuse our desires with a desire for control and then turn every part of our home life upside down so we can look like the other families who seemingly have it all together.

Desire, birthed in humility, will reap the greatest harvests.

Desire, birthed in humility, will reap the greatest harvests. I have learned this through and through and will never stop reminding myself. So when my control over our family time in the Word of God turned my marriage upside down, and my emotions manipulated my husband to lead in a way that was unnatural to him, our structure began to look different and not so very honoring to God.

Owning Our Role and Embracing It

What happened to turn my heart back to God and my finger-pointing away from the builder? I was convicted to own my role in creating a personal, relational, and beautiful time with my children. I realized that with the time I have with my children, there was no good reason I couldn't get into the Word with them by myself.

I picked up my Bible, borrowed a children's Bible study book, and snuggled up on the couch with my children and we read the Word. This grew into a creative time of singing, role playing, trivia, worship, Bible memorization, and more as the years have passed. This is now our favorite time of the day together! It is not perfect. I have had little ones at my breast, toddlers hanging upside down on the couch cushions, eager to be finished, and teens sighing and wondering if they will ever be allowed to outgrow our time together. But because we have pushed through, the days have turned into years and this spiritual discipline has become a part of our DNA and our legacy—so much that if we were to stop, I think there would be an all-out panic. We love our time together. We have read through the same devotional book about 20 times, learned the Bible heroes, the attributes of God, theology, and everything in between, because a small daily habit has turned into a passion to know more of Jesus.

Truth to Live By

Listen, dear friends, to God's truth,
bend your ears to what I tell you.
I'm chewing on the morsel of a proverb;
I'll let you in on the sweet old truths,
Stories we heard from our fathers,
counsel we learned at our mother's knee.
We're not keeping this to ourselves,
we're passing it along to the next generation—
GOD's fame and fortune,
the marvelous things he has done.
(Psalm 78:1-4 MSG)

We are not perfect; we are also not pious. I left that behind on the cross when I owned my responsibility to feed my children the meat and not just the milk of the Word. To this day, I thank the Lord for His conviction in this area. When I think of all the time I had wasted pining away at what should be, rather than what could be, I realize how quickly the years go by and how I should seize the moments.

Taking the Steps

Is it time for you to own your personal role in giving the Word of God to your children in bite-sized portions? What do you feel you need to do to get this rolling and make it your own? You don't need to feel intimidated or alone in this. Let's begin here together. I always find great encouragement knowing someone else has blazed a trail of trial and error before me. I will share some starting points and ideas here for you to start today! How exciting to think that our children don't need to wait one more day to see the Word of God come alive in their homes!

Bite-Sized Beginnings

God's Word is not intimidating. It is our fear of not bringing it alive for our children that stalls us. God's Word is quick and active (Hebrews 4:12). He will do the work. Just lead in obedience.

Choose one verse per week to memorize as a family.

After steady progress, begin adding more verses into to your memory time.

Make up hand motions for your memory verses.

Use rhythms, songs, flashcards, or other creative ideas to help the words stick.

Sing out of a praise book or a hymnal or listen to a worship CD.

Use age-appropriate devotional study Bibles for your children.

Start small and add more time and content as you and they are comfortable.

Add in Bible trivia.

Add in "Sword Drills" (a simple contest search for verses) as a family.

Always read from your Bible, even when using other materials.

Repeat verses for emphasis.

Ask questions and give your children practical application ideas.

Have your children read verses out loud.

Talk about a verse that encourages serving others. Then do ministry as a family.

Use nature as a catalyst for your topic choices.

Use a conflict in your home as a study from the Word.

Be flexible with your timing but consistent with your commitment.

Give little ones grace and wiggle room. Let them enjoy time in the Word.

Illustrate and color the Bible stories and display the art.

Use holidays to spend more time in focused passages of Scripture.

Keep journals and encourage your children to journal and take notes.

Help them find passages in their own Bibles and ask them to follow along.

Use maps to learn where Bible stories take place.

Get your kids moving; it will help the learning process.

My Parenting Principle

It is my responsibility to give my children the Word of God and the truths to live by. I have a captive audience, so I will be intentional and seize the opportunities given to me. When I choose to embrace my role in giving my kids the everyday truth in a fun, relatable, practical, and applicable way, my world will be transformed from a me-centered family to a gospel-centered family!

Lord, I don't want to blame others anymore for my children's lack of sensitivity to Your Word. I don't want to pass the baton of responsibility to someone else to have devotions with them. Will You guide me in this and help me find the courage and strength to begin or to continue? If there is opposition or doubt, I am asking You to grant me peace in knowing that I could never go wrong in giving my kids the tools You provide for life. I trust You, Jesus, and I want more than anything to model obedience to my kids. Help us in this endeavor and life habit. In Jesus' name, amen.

18

{WHY}
A Tired Mom Can Be the Most Influential Mom

Honestly, I hemmed and hawed over this title. It can be difficult to consider our tiredness and humanness as a tool for God's influence. But a shift in how we see our weakness makes all the difference.

While I consider myself to be independent and full of creativity and fortitude, I have realized some of my greatest weaknesses are causing strong, impenetrable walls to form between others and my real and raw needs. If we view our exhaustion or our needs as a crack in our independence or consider ourselves to be "less of a woman" because of them, then those protective walls we build will always be a barrier to our growth. And our children's growth.

Many of us don't trust others enough to let them in, ask for help, or admit to our need to rest. We worry about judgement and comparison. We hide the real and the raw because we would rather deal with the outcome than listen to criticism. I get this through and through.

The tide of independence that has helped women explore their purposes and talents has also caused some backlash. More or different expectations have been placed on our shoulders. Sometimes we are the ones inventing those expectations. And along the way toward assurance and purpose, we seem to have labeled the need for help as weakness. This instills shame in our hearts each time we face a struggle or find ourselves stumbling along. Our response?

We hide the real and the raw because we would rather deal with the outcome than listen to criticism.

Many of us have become isolationists who turn from our true need for others in our lives. We are exhausted, and we are hiding it well.

What lesson are we giving to our children for their future if we are not able to teach them it's okay to not have it all together? The very thing we are keeping our children from witnessing could be one of the greatest lessons we share with them: We aren't meant to do life only in our own power.

There is strength in our need. When we are at our lowest mentally, physically, and spiritually, we retreat, collapse, and call on someone or something to help us fix our situation. We make a new plan, and while we wait for renewed energy, God is at the forefront of our minds, words, prayers, and pleas. We ask for help, we realize we need Him more than anything and anyone, and we bring our faith back to the basics—and our family follows.

Raising daughters afforded me many opportunities to train my girls to be brave, bold, independent, strong, responsible women. As I continue in this daily investment, I have realized that my early motherhood was missing an ingredient. I had forgotten to teach my girls the value of rest and the gift of help. Raising my children brought me to my knees in sheer exhaustion, both mental and physical, wondering if I would ever survive the rigorous daily routine before me. Crawling into bed at night, listening for their cries, only to get back up a few hours later was my call for all these years. Add this to every other responsibility I have as a mom, and the scales were not tipped in my favor for mothering strong. I was worn out, and I kept pushing through.

My weakest moments in my motherhood can be the catalyst to my children seeking God's strength and seeing His power. When we keep our needs separated from our children, then how will they know our true source of strength? Our children can see us draw closer to God in the most difficult situations, but we need to allow them to know the true Redeemer in all of our pain and weakness.

- If our children cannot see God at work in their own homes, then how will they learn to lean on Him when they leave our safe spaces?

- If our children cannot serve one another and bear burdens of those closest to them, then how will they live out this biblical principle later in life?

- If our children do not see our need and reliance on God, will they grow up to be overwhelmed adults, forgetting who can rescue them from their lowest moments?

- If we pretend to have it all together, how will our children know who really holds us together?

God is our Redeemer, Rescuer, Sustainer and Strong Tower. He is the only reason we bear the name mother. Let's call on His Name and reflect His presence in our lowest moments. This is where His glory shines brighter. We want our children to see more of Him and less of us.

My weakest moments in my motherhood can be the catalyst to my children seeking God's strength and seeing His power.

Let Them See and Know

For two years, I struggled with a chronic illness that was out of my control and required weekly medical intervention to manage. This affected my energy, my strength, and my motherhood. I was tired and weak and had to lay aside everything. Everything I did for my family had to be put on hold. This wrecked me to the core. I felt like I was abandoning my post. I experienced feelings of guilt and anger over those things that limited my motherhood or made me feel weak, weary, and incapable. I began to resent the very thing that could open my children's eyes (and mine) and allow God's grace and strength to hold us up and be enough for right then and right now.

I never told my children the truth about my physical trials. For more than a year, I received treatments and pushed through my limitations. I preserved my brave exterior, yet I wasn't able to do all the things I once did, and my motherhood had to take a backseat to my rest and healing. My children deserved to know, because I needed their help and God wanted to use this. I was getting in the way of receiving His grace, their help, and understanding.

The Value of Resting and Reaching Out

If there was one thing I would have ever changed in my motherhood, it would be this: I would have shared my weaknesses and asked for help. I would have been honest with my kids when I was worn thin and could barely hang on. I would have put a halt to our activities and set aside times for rest. I would have allowed my children to see the real and the raw.

Thankfully, God gave me a few rounds of child raising, and I have now come to understand the value of allowing my children into my weary and worn places as I mother this next generation. The builder often tells me that our children cannot understand the emotions behind our parenting until they can see the moments propelling our movements. Our late nights, work deadlines, sickness, marriage stressors, and more are a few of the examples we live in daily as adults that our children do not understand or see.

You will expand your children's understanding of your need for God's help and that of others when you allow them to know how much sleep you didn't have. Show them your schedule and ask for grace. Give them a sense of your external commitments, those things that may pull on your time and cannot be eliminated. Our children don't need to live out the concerns of our adult world, but we can give them a bigger picture of the pressing in of our commitments. Our point is not to burden them or cause them to feel our stress or exhaustion, but to show a gentle patience or added grace with us when we tell them where we are in our lives. As mothers, our open communication with our children is not to be in the form of negativity or complaining, but a word of honesty and a request for an added measure of longsuffering, understanding, or the ability to take a step away and breathe.

Do not hide your tired, weary bones from your praying friends, from your children, and especially from God. He knew this was coming before we even got here. He was waiting for us to call out for rest and renewed strength. The beauty in our weakness is His glory and His strength. Don't shut the door on your shortcomings. Allow your children to see that you need God more than anyone or anything else. Nothing is more cementing for faith than seeing dependence in action. Let them see God show up when you are worn down.

Show God's Glory

To have a strong and healthy relationship with your children, it is vital to bring them along with you emotionally. Often we hold up a strong facade in hopes that our children will not see us in our lowest, weakest moments.

We want them to be strong, to learn from us, and to know that we can rely on God as our strong tower. If we are open and honest with ourselves and our children, they are able to see all the work God is doing in and for us. Don't hide the glory of His power and redemption from your children. This is what faith is all about. Ask your children for prayer and an added measure of love. If your children are still little, go easy on yourself and forget about being the hero and the glue that holds everything together.

Truth to Live By

Trust in the LORD with all your heart
and lean not on your own understanding;
in all your ways submit to him,
and he will make your paths straight.
(Proverbs 3:5-6)

We never want our children to see us as a "strong woman," meaning one who doesn't need anyone or anything, while we fall apart at the seams in our private spaces. A truly strong, grace-filled woman loves Jesus more than her pride and allows others to be a part of her journey, while she leads and loves those around her with His strength. Allow your children to walk with you emotionally and spiritually, and give God the credit for the strength you have each day. Sometimes our prayer is just to make it through one more day of motherhood, and that is enough.

Our strength and bravery is a thin veneer hiding our exhaustion and real-life struggles. Getting real and raw with our kids is the first step in asking for grace. Everyday motherhood requires daily prayer and an urgency to know God more. This is the gift you will pass onto your children daily.

Mothers, let your children see you need Jesus!

The Impact of Honesty

Consider with me the values you wish to pass on to the next generation. Carry those thoughts into bite-sized daily lessons for your own children. Your example is the model they will use to transfer these lessons into their own lives. When our daughters see us put on a brave face and give more to everyone around us while barely holding on to our sanity and strength, they see a woman without boundaries, void of peace. We want to shine with a deep-seated peace in our callings. Motherhood does not have to be drudgery or a source of pride, throughout which we carry the banner of independence and espouse a false message of "doing it all." When we are honest and truthful about our circumstances, we allow an infusion of hope and help into our worlds.

Perhaps you're thinking your little ones will never understand the labor and energy you invest in their lives on a daily basis. You can present it in a way that they will comprehend. Honesty may sound like, "No, we cannot go anywhere today," or "Mommy will take a nap when you take yours and dinner will be spur of the moment." Honesty will be expressed to our older children in truthful words, emotions, and gentle explanations of why we will turn down certain commitments or why the family will have to change a few things for a while.

If we were willing to be a little bit more honest with our schedules, commitments and our need for one another, then we wouldn't feel as much shame and women would feel more comfortable in their own skin.

Taking the Steps

There is so much grace afforded to us, but we often miss it because we have confused independence with strength. God gives us strength, and we can rely on others to bear our burdens when we cannot. To raise children who will know how to seek God and the wisdom of others, we can be the example to them in our motherhood.

Here are some guidelines and truths I found to be helpful:

1. Let others in. Often we doubt the intentions of others and our skepticism or mistrust puts up walls that may need tearing down. Pray that God will give you the ability and discernment to allow others to help you, bear your burdens, and give you wisdom.

2. Be real and raw. When someone asks how you are, answer them with grace-filled honesty. Not everyone needs to know the nitty-gritty details (kids vomiting, piles of run-on laundry, no time for your shower, or anger toward your husband), but we can tell them the truth. Try this: "I am tired, exhausted, and barely holding it together. Will you pray for me?" Or, "I have no idea why my teenager is so angry, my baby will not sleep through the night, and I have had migraines for the last two weeks. My laundry is piling up, the baby is teething, and my husband wonders why I am so moody and grumpy."

3. Genuine people will show they care. If you are struggling with trusting those around you with the reality of your struggles, questions, or exhaustion, then use this as a discerning tool to help you form a pattern of sharing your burdens with others.

   • When your honesty is reciprocated with prayer, help, verses, wisdom, or confirmation, you can trust those around you.

   • When you experience judgement, gossip, or even comradery with those that want to talk about their own

problems and forget about yours, this is a red flag. Use
grace-filled words and discretion in how much you
share.

4. Do not hide your reality from your children. Have a family
meeting and share the times of extra stress that may be
coming, or sit with your child and share your tears, your
tiredness, and your heart. Ask them to be patient with you
and tell them you are waiting on God and have nothing
else to give right now.

5. Do not expect your children to understand. Your children
won't understand the full scope of the concerns you face
as an adult, but that isn't the lesson and wisdom they
are supposed to glean from you. The spiritual growth
will occur when they see you in your weakest moments,
giving everything to God and allowing Him to show His
supernatural strength in your lives. Honesty is the open
door to growth.

What do you have to hide? If you're trying to cover your tired eyes,
your weary bones, and your words with something other than the truth,
what will your children know about life and leaning into Jesus? The
tired mom can be the most influential mom, because God shines His
redemption in everything through a lens of honesty and truth. Mama,
please do not hide your financial stress, your long, tired nights, or your
worry over the future from your children. I used to feel like I was complaining and grumbling and this would be all my children ever remembered of me. I was reminded that a truly strong and brave woman will
let others in and allow God to shine His will and redemption in her life.
My influence depends on my honesty.

My Parenting Principle

A mother who admits her weariness is not a weak woman. My
influence will be as strong as my ability to allow my children to see
God's grace working in my life. I will work on allowing others into

my space and accepting help. I will ask for prayer and share my burdens with those I can trust. My exhaustion and weariness is not to be resented, nor should I be ashamed of where I am in this season. God redeems my moments when I let Him. I will allow my children insight into my own story and allow them to practice grace for their mama.

Lord, I am tired and weary and I feel quite alone in this. Do other women get stuck here? And who do they ask for help? I am asking for discernment and guidance. Will You help me find the words to be real and send women into my life who can walk through this with me? I need this now more than ever. Your grace is sufficient, Lord. I believe this. Sometimes, I know, You will be the only one I can talk to about this, and I trust You with my weariness and my honesty. You are my Redeemer. I trust in You. In Jesus' name, amen.

19

{WHY}
Our Children Should Serve
(Even When It Is Uncomfortable)

I am convinced I am the meanest mom on this planet. You too?

No one wants to be the rule maker, the fun breaker, the lesson planner, the enforcer, and the coercer all at the same time.

We just want to be Mom. Period.

And yet those identities are us, and that is the job: Motherhood in all its glory.

The around-the-clock work, prayer, guilt, and grime of motherhood requires guts, and it results in very little glory. It demands bravery, fortitude, and resolve. I promise you your work will reap rewards, but it takes hard-knuckled, grace-filled, heart-shaping effort and not just wishful thinking or misplaced ideals. I would tell you this in person, and I will tell you here: The hardest part of motherhood is teaching your children to be like Jesus and serve others when you are still learning yourself.

How We See Others

When my firstborn son was a baby, we were a two-man show. The builder worked insanely long hours and we still hadn't figured out any form of balance in our lives. Our transportation was limited to one car, and I chose the short straw and stayed home day after day with hours of free time on my hands and an active, contagiously happy baby. You can only clean your home from top to bottom so many times, play piano tunes for your music-loving little one, read books, go for walks, make new recipes, and write letters before the list of creative ideas comes to a screeching halt. One day, when I sat on our rickety wooden front steps with my son on my lap, watching the traffic, I noticed the bigger world in front of me. We had houses across the highway, another family up the road, and people travelling up and down our busy intersection daily. This was a mission field, and I had finally burst out of my baby world to see the ministry right in front of us this whole time.

Truth to Live By

Work willingly at whatever you do, as though you were working for the Lord rather than for people.
(Colossians 3:23 NLT)

I had everything timed perfectly. The banana bread was cooling, the baby had been bathed, hair combed all cute, his hat and coat by the door along with a vase of flowers we had picked from my small flower garden. We had a plan and it was a go.

Carefully maneuvering the baby on my hip and the basket of food and flowers in my other hand, we walked down our hill to cross the busy highway. We had chosen the brown-and-yellow trailer as our first place to spread good cheer and say hello.

After knocking with a nervous timidity, I heard a dog barking on the other side of the steel door and a few gruff voices travel loudly from one end of the paper-thin walls of the trailer. There was scuffling and rearranging, and the front curtain pulled back long enough for me to know someone might answer the door.

The woman who pulled open the door was small in frame and as tired as I have ever seen another person. Her smile was weak and she waited for me to speak. It didn't take long for me to realize that I was going to have to invite myself in. And I did. My baby boy and I sat at her tiny table and ate banana bread together. A few men and two children dared to stray into our presence long enough for me to gain a better understanding of what this woman's daily life might be like. The air was thick with smoke, and their dogs were large, present, and intimidating. She lit up her cigarette and then, rather quickly and with apparent embarrassment, put it out as she looked at my son.

So much for the baby's bath and the consideration of appearances. Those weren't pressures in this home. Our initial interaction was rather awkward, but I pushed through. Everyone knows that a baby makes a great conversation piece. I noticed a little light shine through her countenance and a smile curving her lips when she asked to hold the baby. Out the window went my standards for germs and health for our son. I handed him over slowly and she held him fondly and bounced him; her joy was so beautiful. He seemed blissfully happy to be held and appreciated by her. As our conversation came to an end, she thanked me for the vase of flowers, the bread, and most of all, our visit. We walked to the door together, and her kids came running to say goodbye with their ceremonious energy and eagerness. The wooden frame to the door was loose, so I carefully stepped down the last step to their lawn and then made my way back across the highway. My mind rushed through the details of our visit and caused a stirring in me that set the pace for the rest of my motherhood years.

With every baby born, I found new adventures for us that required us to move out of our comfort zones, meet new people, and discover there are people who do not know the true love of Jesus. Our children learned to see others, their differences, and their problems as Jesus sees them. Their eyes became opened to others' needs and grew blind to their differences.

How we see others will be how our children see others.

Break Down the Barriers

Motherhood doesn't just happen in the walls of your home. It doesn't always mean diaper changes, homework, groceries, errands, and needs. Motherhood will require us to teach the hardest lesson of all. Our children will never be able to serve the Lord or others in any relationship until they learn to put others first. The selfless act of serving is more than just actions as a means to an end. Serving others requires us to bow our own desires low, to bring our hearts to a place of humility, and to not allow our weaknesses or excuses to get in the way. So how do we draw our children out of their shells, and encourage them to serve others with their whole heart and put away judging when it is easy to see the differences? Motherhood calls us to teach our children to serve even when it is uncomfortable.

Often we are unaware of the unique culture we have created within the walls of our homes. The way you think, talk, act, and interact as a family will be the very culture your children expect and will bring to the world around them. It is our job as mothers to draw out the heart of Jesus in our children, focusing on their strengths in serving and seeing others, and working on their unique weaknesses to expose the areas that might be barriers when it comes to serving others.

> Our children will never be able to serve the Lord or others in any relationship until they learn to put others first.

Some children are shy, introverted, and uncomfortable with new people. They need an extra nudge of confidence and encouragement to keep their personalities from getting in the way of serving others.

Some children are outspoken, with strong opinions—spokespeople who have difficulty doing anything that might not be fun or entertaining, or where they may not be the center of attention. They will need direction, correction, and training to see that their gifts can be used for leadership, but true humility comes in serving others.

Those children who are complainers or easily discouraged and not prone to doing anything out of their comfort zone may dig their heels into the ground. They need a strong nudge along with daily work in doing things they do not like and learning that life is not all about them.

Perhaps this sounds overwhelming, the thought of so many personalities and so much work to teach them how to serve. This is the kind of roll-up-your-sleeves, put-on-your-brave-heart, daily work of training that will matter when your children are all grown up.

Do the Work Daily

Selfish adults are raised as selfish children. Your daily, life-learning lessons will help form children's strengths and weaknesses into traits of loving, caring, selfless adults. They won't be perfect, but thinking and seeing others through a lens of love is possible. Is your home characterized by the "me-first" syndrome, complaining, and ungrateful spirits? Is conversation about others and their faults? Is your sole motherhood ministry *to* your children and not *for* your children?

Ministry *to* your children means your focus is on serving them with God's love but not necessarily showing them the way to do the same. Motherhood is a ministry *for* your children. For their hearts, their future, and for others. Your children will someday minister to others. Will they know how?

For three straight years, the children and I packed our backpacks, snacks, water bottles, the diaper bag, and music books and headed to the nursing homes for a weekly visit with the residents who became our dear friends. As cheery as this sounds, it didn't begin as easily as I had hoped, and it took weeks of encouragement, grace, and teaching in our home and in the presence of the residents for my children to be comfortable with their visits. It was not a forced activity, but a sweet, grace-filled learning process of drawing out and giving from their individual gifts.

I will never forget the first week I pulled our 15-passenger van into the narrow parking lot of the nursing home and the kids looked up to the dismal brick building with awe and fear. After the tedious process of pairing them up as buddies and double checking our bags for tiny details, we held hands, crossed the street, and opened the wide, heavy front doors to a whole new world.

> Motherhood is a ministry *for* your children.

I watched my children peer with fear and timidity up and down the halls and then back at me in wonder. Without speaking, they were saying, "What are we going to do here?" Lining the halls were wheelchairs with older men and women bent over talking to one another, crying for help, or yelling at imaginary people. It was so warm in the building, I had to unbundle the baby and strip layers off the kids.

The kids stood motionless. I gently encouraged them to follow me to the gathering room, where a television played loudly and residents sat scattered in rows and circles. It was apparent there would be a strong distinction between those who were aware of their life in the nursing home, and those who had no memory of or clarity in their current life. This was the first time my children had been in the presence of so many different people. Gray hair, balding, no teeth, some teeth. Some were mumbling, some talking loudly, and some were smiling, friendly and encouraging to the children.

We rallied our senses, pulled our music books out of our bags, and began the first of many visits to serve others and put our comfort last. As my 11-year-old son sat down at the old piano and began to play songs for the residents, the other children and I stood in the middle of the crowd and sang. What began as a whisper grew to be a chorus after three years of ministering in music to our new friends at the nursing home.

Truth to Live By

"You are the salt of the earth. But if the salt loses its saltiness, how can it be made salty again? It is no longer good for anything, except to be thrown out and trampled underfoot. You are the light of the world. A town built on a hill cannot be hidden. Neither do people light a lamp and put it under a bowl. Instead they put it on its stand, and it gives light to everyone in the house."
(Matthew 5:13-15 NIV)

We made our weekly trek to the old brick building every week for three years. The children formed many dear friendships and loved those residents with everything in them. We began notebooks for each resident so the kids could record the residents' thoughts and life stories. The children would play checkers and cards and sing music to these new friends. No longer strangers to serving out of their comfort zone and befriending people who were different from them, my children grew to love those they used to fear. Fear in serving only creates distance between your children and knowing the true reward of loving others more than ourselves.

Did we have to step out of our comfort zone? Yes.

Did I go home exhausted and wonder what in the world had possessed me to do this weekly? Yes.

Were there tough moments when my children didn't want to serve or do the hard thing? Yes.

Did my children resent me for making them do this? No.

Mothers soften and mold hearts at home so their children can allow God to work in and through them when she is not in control. Serving is not rooted in requirement. It does not call for demands or control. It is an outpouring of the people they are to become.

Taking the Steps

Once your heart tells your mind it's okay for your children to be uncomfortable while they are serving, that's when the Holy Spirit takes over and lives are transformed. "Give it to God," I tell my children when they realize that I cannot make something easier or better for them, but they know it's the right thing.

What do we do when our kids are hesitant or downright grumbling about serving others? We do it with them again and again, until the joy of giving out and giving back is so overwhelming, it takes hold of their hearts. Remind yourself to go easy on your kids when you begin stepping into new areas to bring Jesus to people. Serving isn't easy at first because it is where our faith is our walk and more than our talk. Let your kids know that Jesus is glorified when they say yes to trying. That's all we ask when things are hard, right?

Here are some ideas to help you and your family get started:

- Create handwritten notes for neighbors, family members, or strangers.
- Deliver kindness (baked goods, notes, flowers) to others.
- Practice random acts of kindness.
- Serve in church ministries.
- Carry groceries for others.
- Read to the elderly.

- Put carts away in parking lots.
- Visit nursing homes.
- Use unique gifts to minister to others (music, art, talking, baking, reading).
- Learn to pray at home and in public for others.

My Parenting Principle

It is my job to show my children what the hands and feet of Jesus look like. When I encourage my children to serve with their strengths and their weaknesses, it allows them to see that anyone who has given his or her life to Him can serve, despite their fears and their faults. When I am comfortable sacrificing and showing up, my children will see others through the lens I give them. I will open their eyes with compassion and care and give them the gift of serving unconditionally.

Dear Abba Father, You know my heart and my desire to show others who You are to me, but I desperately desire for my kids to have a passion for shining You in their own lives. Help me, Lord, to be a walking, breathing example of loving others and seeing them as You do. Help me to step out in confidence to do the work and to lead my children in humility and grace to serve others, even when it isn't comfortable. In Jesus' name, amen.

20

{WHY}
Ministry and Mission Should Happen as a Family

The new revelation for women is to find their purpose. There is a rise in women's hunger to identify their callings and to group with others on a similar path and to join the pursuit of the mission they think they are missing. I am all about purpose, my identity, and my calling. But when we are given children, our purpose and mission field and our identity begins there. If at any time our passions take us away from this, and our ministry to and with them becomes second, I'm afraid we are teaching our children that our personal pursuits in ministry are more important than their hearts. I am not referring to putting yourself second or having a child-centered home; I am straight-talking about ministry here. In the name of Jesus, what will you go after the most?

Why does motherhood matter? Because you matter to God, and the hearts of your children should matter to you. If we lose sight of our first mission as moms, then every day will be filled with tiring, repetitive actions. The mundane will drown out the blessings and our passion for their little lives will grow weaker, as they grow older and bigger and our influence doesn't seem to matter as much.

Seize the Moments and the Days

With ten children, one still in diapers and the oldest having graduated high school, I knew that my ministry could be for my children and with my children, while maintaining my priorities as well. With a lot of prayer over those activities I would take on outside of my home, I followed the Holy Spirit and allowed Him to give my children and me special assignments for our daily investments. Some areas we scheduled into our days, and with others we allowed Him to give us direction.

That hot, cloudy day in July, when I had the oven set at 350 degrees and 6 loaves of banana bread baking, completely and utterly transformed me. Many times I would senselessly bake bread or cookies or buy random gifts, knowing God had already picked out the recipient. When the kids asked who the treat was for, I told them that we wouldn't know until it was time. There was a day when I would have considered it ridiculous to heat up the oven on a hot summer day, but I have learned to not listen to reason when it comes to serving.

Banana bread out of the oven and wrapped, packed, and loaded for delivery, all ten kids and I boarded our big van and headed down our hill into town. I let the kids choose where to stop and who to give the bread to. It was always handed over with a smile and a blessing and nothing too flowery, other than, "The Lord told us to bake this for you and we hope it blesses you."

Five loaves down and one loaf left, we drove for more than ten minutes around town, through neighborhoods and into the park, and then we began to turn for home. We had a full-blown diaper change on the side of the road, a little meltdown sparked by the heat of the day, and restless kids ready to call it a day. That is the reality of serving as a family. But, thankfully, the Lord never leaves us there.

I have learned to not listen to reason when it comes to serving.

As I passed through our town, I felt burdened to slow down directly in front of our church. The home that sits across the highway from our small-town church was a scene of interest for us for many years. Every time the church doors were opened, the owner of that home could be seen sitting in his driveway in a lawn chair, with a large beverage in hand and sunglasses perched on his nose. He would watch us come and go. Go and come. His routine was as predictable as ours.

He began to wave back to us when we dared say hello and we even stopped once in a while to invite him and his family over for an event or services. But, in our heart of hearts, it wasn't church that we were inviting him to; it was the gospel. The walking, living, breathing Word of God that we can all live and share.

On this day of banana bread deliveries, there was not a lawn chair in sight. In fact, the house looked locked up and quiet. But I pulled into his sloped driveway in our big van full of hot, tired and now very restless children. Tingles of doubt began to creep up my spine. I sent one of the kids to the door, with instructions to leave the bread on the front step with a note. They knocked instead. No answer. They knocked again, missing my attempt at waving them back to the van. This time, the door slowly opened and my child just stood there. This moment is forever frozen on my mind. The man stood silently, unmoving on the other side of his screen door and my child just stared back, motionless. What my son did next stunned me. He held out his hands with the bread and spoke the words, "We brought this to you, because Jesus told us to and because He loves you."

The screen door opened quickly, the serious onlooker took the bread gently and proceeded to walk right up to my van window. He stood again motionless. I have never felt so helpless in ministering to another person. I didn't know if he was angry, offended, or confused.

He stood there quietly as I tried to stammer out a few words of kindness and wishes for his day while waving my hand frantically behind my back at the children who had begun to argue. Their bantering came to a halt when they noticed the man was crying. Crying tears that rolled down from behind his sunglasses. He could barely talk. I was attempting to find words about the banana bread and the nice summer day when I suddenly felt led to just be still. To be quiet and to wait. He told me that he had just returned home from the cemetery. They had buried his twin grandsons, born too early, and the sorrow of the good-bye was more than he could audibly voice to me. He leaned in close and asked me to pray for his daughter, for him.

Truth to Live By

Blessed are the poor in spirit,
  for theirs is the kingdom of heaven.
Blessed are those who mourn,
  for they will be comforted.
Blessed are the meek,
  for they will inherit the earth.
(Matthew 5:3-5 NIV)

Broken into a million little pieces in this man's driveway is how God works. This very day, 18 years to the moment, I delivered twin baby boys and buried them with a deep grief I never thought would go away. God is in the business of healing and using our stories to redeem His plan and our pain. This was the day I could confidently say to this hurting man, "I know this pain well. I understand and I want to and will pray for you. I am so deeply sorry."

Our eyes locked in the middle of that divine appointment. The banana bread was lost in the moment, and my children were mesmerized by God's big plan for such a small errand.

Motherhood matters when your children can learn ministry with you.

Taking the Steps

When was the last time you stepped outside your comfort zone to listen to God's leading to follow and serve Him? Now, consider when you might have ministered locally as a family. In our day-to-day lives, we lose sight of the needs around us. We think we need to take a big mission trip or organize an event to make this happen. We don't. We have a wide-open canvas of opportunity right in front of us. It's what we do with it that matters. Why include our children? Mothers often complain that they are limited in their ministry because of their children and their schedules or needs. You and your children are the answer to the question, "How can we serve the Lord while in this season of life?" Begin together and watch Him direct your steps.

My Parenting Principle

If reaching into the hearts of my children is so vitally important to my mission, then I must realize that part of that space should include serving others. We want our children to love Jesus more than anything, but they will need to learn to put others first before their lives can be fully used by Him. When we serve and minister as a family, hypocrisy is absent and our children learn from our humility and our courage. I want the next generation to be obedient listeners, to me and to their heavenly Father. I am their primary example of listening, loving, and leading.

Lord, often I feel secluded and ashamed that I cannot do more for You as a Christ-follower. You know my heart and I want to serve, but I feel like my mission field at home gets in the way of any ministry. Help me to change my perspective, Lord. Will You help me to be open-minded and to see the plan You have for my kids and me every day? I need courage and confidence. I am asking for help to put away my excuses and my selfish choices about where and whom I serve. Help our family to minister together. I pray for our unity and a fresh joy in reaching out from our self-centered lives. In Jesus' name, amen.

21

{WHY}
Memorizing Scripture
Will Change Lives

The curly, soft, blond hair and his enthusiastic and loving smile won me over more times than I care to admit. Our firstborn son and I had endless hours of creative learning, adventures, ministry, and meeting people. He was rarely a naughty or mischievous child, and so he rarely had to be spoken to sternly about anything. Mama, there is a difference between speaking to our children about their behavior and addressing and correcting it. A change in behavior will require time, intervention, explanation of *why* a behavior is inappropriate, and teaching on *how* to change.

As my boy grew more independent and opinionated, I realized there were areas in which he needed correction that I had not tended to early on, hoping to never see the problem repeated. He was a talker and because it was often just the two of us, it was quite nice to have his little voice fill the air. But after a few weeks of memorizing the Word to music, we had a recurrence of his uncontrolled tongue in action. He continually interrupted, spoke over me, or used his tongue in a negative way to complain, whine, or say unkind things to his new little sister.

I learned that it is so much easier to expect behavioral changes and be happy with that, as long as we are not continually affected by the inconvenience or embarrassment of their problem. Yet, unless the root of a problem is traced back to the heart, you will see the behavior pop back up time and again, because roots can grow deep. I was faced with more questions than answers when it came to applying this principle.

How do I know the root of my child's behavior? Where do I begin? How can I help him overcome this?

Trusting God's Word to Transform

My search began for wisdom in this area. I asked friends, I read books, read the Bible, and asked some more. After weeks of struggling with my adorable little boy's problem, I realized the answer was before me the whole time: The put-off, put-on principle I had applied to my own life when I desired change or growth.

This is when I placed my trust in memorizing God's Word to have the power to put his problem into perspective, even when my words were not enough to correct the behavior.

We began to put small verses of Scripture to memory. My surprise came with the shocking realization that my little boy's mind was capable of committing a lot more to memory than I would've anticipated. Every day, we made it a fun experience to say our verses. It wasn't for show, or for points, or for church. It was for us. Our hearts.

Truth to Live By
Seek first the kingdom of God and His righteousness, and all these things shall be added to you.
(Matthew 6:33 NKJV)

I hope you're not imagining God's Word to be a magic pill. Not at all. When our little guy had a problem, I would address it and ask him to think of a verse we had learned together about the tongue or our words. He would think hard, sometimes humming through his verses, until he recalled one that suited the situation. I had him say the verse again. Then we would replace the pronouns in the verse with his name and he would repeat it again. Next, we would think of a verse about the negative effects the tongue can have. He was five years old, and he understood this and appreciated it. It was a positive daily time we had together, gathering God's Word and making it stick in our minds. The verses made sense because we learned stories and songs related to them. We even drew pictures to bring the words to life. He got it, because the Word was already in his heart.

After a few months we realized the power and influence God's Word had in our home when we took the time to hide it in our hearts. I also realized that when my children have a hardened heart, or when they are struggling with a problem, a stronghold, or something they cannot see, I can pray.

I began to pray verses over my children and their lives. There is no greater relief to a parent then to relinquish control and ownership over a problem our child has that we feel we cannot fix. His Word holds so many promises and so much wisdom. There is no greater gift to give your children than to hide God's Word in their hearts.

Reaping and Sowing

Every single one of us has bad, no-good, wish-we-could-erase motherhood days. It is inevitable. I wish I could say I have motherhood all figured out, but to be honest, I wouldn't trust anyone who said this—and I hope you don't either. Here is the thing we can remember: If we didn't have bad moments, rough days, and frustration over run-on sentences, then we wouldn't have the opportunity to rest, change, grow, and reboot. Rebooting is always better when you find a little bright spot in the middle of the drudgery and gloom.

Driving to town, with two kiddos strapped into car seats and in my rearview mirror sight, I was down-in-the-dumps tired and bone weary from everyone and everything. You know those moments that feel monumental, but are really a small inconvenience or something we can overcome. I was there. I let the tears fall freely as we drove. I figured I could see my kids, but they could not see me, and so I grieved my bad day like a champ and let out a little sniffle here and there.

My little tow-headed singer called to me from his car seat.

"Are you crying, Mommy? Are you sad?"

"No. Maybe. I don't know. I'll be okay, buddy."

"Mommy, don't you remember?"

"No?"

"Remember?"

Hmmmm...Sniff. "No."

"'This is the day the LORD has made; we will rejoice and be glad in it.'"

I had to pull the car over. This little boy had been learning Psalms for a few weeks and this verse, 118:24, was relevant to him and his mommy right now. How did he know the application, the verse, and when to use it? How?

Truth to Live By

So is my word that goes out from my mouth: It will not return to me empty, but will accomplish what I desire and achieve the purpose for which I sent it.
(Isaiah 55:11 NIV)

The three of us sat in the car parked on the side of the road and sang this verse until my tears were overcome by awe, joy, and thankfulness that my five-year-old could change my perspective with the power of his Bible memory verses. It was real to him. Real, relied on, and relayed. This is the power of memorizing Scripture with your children. Never underestimate the ability of your children's minds to memorize, and never discriminate against their ability to use the power of the Word because they are children.

More Than Knowledge

Knowledge is vital. But knowledge without love and application is empty. Knowledge puffs up and will leave us void of change and conviction. If we don't know God and who He is, our lives will lead to destruction. When we know God and our knowledge is paired with His love, then it will bear fruit.

We have so many opportunities to train up our children in the Word. They may learn Bible stories and Bible verses, go to church and Sunday school, and do and say the "right things." May I appeal to you that there is more? There is a why to their walk and their talk. We can

There is
no greater gift
to give your children
than to hide
God's Word
in their hearts.

help lead them and show them daily how to live our lives by His Word and not just add it to the list of things to do.

Motherhood is a wide-open invitation to living a life led and loved by Jesus. Our children need to know why. Otherwise they'll go looking someplace else. Let them see you live out the Word in your life. Your life will be the first walking, talking example of God's love they will remember. Be sure to live it.

Taking the Steps

We often mistake our time spent teaching as just another sacrifice for our children, but really, we are the ones blessed in the end. The benefits of teaching Scripture to your children far outweigh the time and work you will put in when they are young. Don't forget that you are learning right along with them, and every verse you have put to memory or covered with your kiddos is another morsel of wisdom to draw from when correcting character, addressing behavior, or encouraging your kids daily. This time also reaps the benefit of applying it to your own lives. The Word of the Lord is alive and active. It comes back to your mind, from the recesses of your memory, when you need it. I can promise you it will never return void.

Let's begin small. I like to use the approach of breaking Scripture into smaller portions. The chart below is just a suggested plan and a starting point for your kids. This will look different for every family, but the key is application. Remember, knowledge alone puffs up, but knowledge with the love and wisdom of Christ will transform.

	Weekly Work	Application	Song/Music	Rhymes	Hand Motions	Flashcards	Repetition	Sign Language	Other Tools
Matthew 5:1-11									
1 John 1									
Fruit of the Spirit									
Armor of God									
Books of the Old Testament									
Books of the New Testament									
James 1									
Romans 12									
Psalm 1									
Matthew 6:33									
Matthew 7:12									

	Weekly Work	Application	Song/Music	Rhymes	Hand Motions	Flashcards	Repetition	Sign Language	Other Tools
John 3:16									
John 14:6									
Proverbs 15:1									
Proverbs 3:1-11									
Psalm 119:1-3									
Psalm 23									
Psalm 34:14									
Galatians 5:22-23									

My Parenting Principle

The greatest gift I can give my child is the Word. God's Word, in their hearts and minds, will stay with them forever. Investing time to memorize Scripture with my children is an eternal gift. An eternal education. Bible memory can be creative, not a formal task robbed of joy and eagerness. Children don't realize the quantity of their learning while they're enjoying the quality. I will embrace this journey with my children and pursue creative and enjoyable ways for us to learn together.

God, You have promised Your Word will be life. You have given us every tool we need in Your Word. Yet memorizing has been a challenge for me. I want to lead my children in learning and memorizing, but I know I cannot do this without You enabling my mind to hold the truth and You helping me be an encouraging and patient teacher to my children. Help us, Lord, to apply Your words to our hearts and to bind them about our necks. Your Word comforts, instructs, guides, and edifies us. Will you grant me the perseverance to apply this to my everyday learning? I want to become like You to put Your words on and share them with my kids. In Jesus' name, amen.

Let's Talk

I am imagining two scenarios here. I know them both quite well, because I have lived them real-time in my living room with other mamas sitting in a circle. When presented with the discussion of leading our children in ministry, the study of God's Word, and dependence on God, some of us were overwhelmed by holding the responsibility for our spiritual lives and for our children's. Others also felt guilty over how they had already missed participating in this holy investment for a portion of their children's lives.

During times of exploring the spiritual roles of being a mom with a group of women, I always break for refreshments at the point when the blessing and the burden sink it. A little bit of chocolate and a cup of hot coffee can help immensely. Every single mom is quiet and contemplating the roots of her spiritual investment in her home. It is such a monumental moment. You might be feeling the significance of this right now.

I placed this exploration further along in our journey together because our faith should be wrapped up in everything we do as a mother. Words can be spent on lists and charts and how-to's. But this is not the kind of mama I am. If your motherhood is viewed through a lens of comparison, riddled with lists and how-to's, then faith will always be the last chapter you remember to read and the last thing on your heart and mind as you mother.

If you were to meet me or my children, I hope that Jesus would shine brighter than my flaws, my helpful hints, or my words. I desire for you to find the truest faith while you walk in your motherhood. It is not a mistake that you are reading with me today. I hope you choose to turn the page to discover a vision for your motherhood that you alone are incapable of creating but are able to shape for your children *with* God's help and strength. Jesus has the bigger picture, far greater than we could ever see for our children. Let Him have the future.

Will you turn the pages with me, with a hope that rests in His promises to sustain us, provide for us, and give us everything we need, especially in our motherhood?

Grab your chocolate and your tea (or coffee) and join me with our circle of other women in exciting steps to discover the very motivation we all need to keep doing this motherhood journey together, every day.

Keep pressing into the words here! We are all in this together.

Part IV

{WHY}
Giving Your Children a Reason to Change Makes All the Difference

I can do everything through Christ, who gives me strength.

PHILIPPIANS 4:13 NLT

22

{WHY}
We Don't Want to Raise Robots

First things first. The builder and I have no desire to raise robots. It doesn't take very long for anyone spending time with our family to notice that every child growing up under this roof is so very, very different. This is not a mistake. We love our children to the moon and back, and not one child feels less loved than another, but they are loved so very differently. We see them as individuals, uniquely fashioned and with special gifts to offer. Therefore we have learned to love them differently, uniquely, and well.

This can be a challenge. I will not pretend that as soon as our first son was placed in our arms we also birthed an instinctive nurturing component to love him uniquely. In fact, it takes a lifetime to figure this out. And this, my friend, is the key to any relationship. Parenting included.

Parenting Their Personality

Consequences of poor behavior are not the same for each child in my home. It has taken much creativity to follow through with our kids as individuals. Often they interpret my instructions differently—my actions mean something completely different to each of them, and their responses are never the same. Parenting to suit each child's uniqueness requires knowledge and longsuffering. I took this seriously as a younger mom. I had to study my children, their strengths, weaknesses, and their love languages, and understand their needs before I could effectively communicate with them. I bet you're thinking, *No way. I don't have time for that!*

May I encourage you to see your children as individuals and treat them the way in which you might wish to be treated? The glorious thing in parenting children like this is that you have one ultimate goal, yet different outcomes. You do not want a stamp of your likeness or a child who makes you happy and your life rosy, cozy, and comfortable. If this is your approach to raising your children, it may seem easier initially, but your result will be a child who grows into an adult who doesn't know who they truly are. They might spend years trying to break free from the mold and discover just *who* God created them uniquely to be.

Please do not confuse this with raising children with total freedom to discover and decide what they will do and when. Your home will require structure, guidance, and the foundation of God's Word for them to know their identity is rooted in something stronger than their individuality.

We should all be ready to give our children the why when their questions arise. This will change their world. There will be so many instances when we will not have the answers to their questions. If everything they do is rooted in their Creator, imagine the difference this will make in your motherhood. It makes it easier! Think about it. You do not have to come up with your own moral guidelines for your home and a fancy reason for why you feel the way you do. Your children will be called to something higher than your authority, so when they leave your home, they are still under His umbrella of wisdom and protection. What a gift the Giver gave us when He said, "I AM" (Exodus 3:14).

Learn to Be a Forward Thinker

I will admit, I have this odd mixture of thrill and excitement when I see another mother discover the golden nugget of truth in parenting with the future in mind. Her motherhood shifts from duty to focus. Frustration and questioning our own methods with tears every day can be minimized when we focus on the why. Every motherhood moment in my day always comes back to one question: How can we learn and grow from this? Sure, there are days I'm exhausted and the last thing I want to focus on is the future and how to make the most of a situation. But the habit of mothering with the future in mind gives us a head start on our reactions to the moments. I often remind my family to act and not react.

We are inclined to desire instant gratification. I will be the first to admit that when I need to repeat the same instruction or the very same request from five minutes ago (or seconds) and my children seem oblivious that there is any sound coming from my mouth, I am quick to react and tell them that their future will be seen from inside their bedroom! Obviously, my children have seen the light of day again, and we are propelling forward together. So take hope and know that as the hardest days hit you full-on, you can learn the habit of thinking forward and acting, rather than reacting, so your own future will seem more doable.

Your children will be called to something higher than your authority, so when they leave your home, they are still under His umbrella of wisdom and protection.

You Are a Team

Tell me if this sounds familiar: You are calmly telling your child that they are unable to have what they want. Your child has a slight bit of defiance in his eyes and his lips are pursed in frustration. He interrupts you with, "But!" You put your hand up and declare that you are not through talking yet, (but really, you are now just repeating the same reasoning in a few different ways) hoping he will see the light. Your voice has raised a notch louder and your speaking pace is a tad bit faster. You *will* get in that last word. Your child is beginning to look agitated and insists you are not listening to him. Now his reasons and his voice seem to rise above your own. This goes on for a little while, until what began as a small talk about one wrong thing has turned into a stream of verbal arguments. Now you have disrespect, anger, truth telling, irresponsibility, rudeness, yelling, and you name it added to the list of things to deal with before you move on with your day. It never ends...until you both throw your hands in the air and walk away, huffing and puffing that neither of you ever listen to one another. You just don't care.

But you do care, and that is why you take up so much mental and emotional energy to get to the bottom of it every single time you need to address something.

If they only knew *how* much we care!

Let me share a little secret with you. Your child walked away with nothing from those moments. Nada. Zilch. Nothing.

You are both saying the same thing. "You never listen and you don't care." But, your hearts are now in two very different places. Far apart.

Give It a Try

Do not be disheartened. Let's imagine the possibilities if a child and a mother were on the same team and not just sounding boards for one another's frustrations. *A team*—two words for two people with one common goal. We are for our children and they trust us in this. Now do we need to figure out how to always keep our cool, be better listeners, not react, and pretty much be perfect? Not at all. We just need to gain a new perspective. You might be thinking this sounds too easy.

To be on the same team will require us to know our child's heart, to ask questions if we don't understand, and to bring every decision or idea back to the truth in God's Word that applies to the situations. When our children can decipher their own decisions through the magnifying glass of God's Word, a lot of their conflict with us disappears. Our moral compass does not need to dictate or stir up conflict. It can always go back to the principles set forth for your family. A mother asking questions and giving her child more to think about than just her opinion will make a greater impact than the mother who responds with a plain no.

It is revolutionary to mother through the lens of the why as we face our life and family matters and even our mistakes. When we approach daily life with an eternal perspective in mind, it cuts a lot of questions and frustration right off the top. It keeps us out of that emotionally elevated place where we can get stuck and seem to run out of oxygen. Our emotions take over and nothing makes sense to either person in that place.

Motherhood is an investment and not a lighthearted commitment to fly by the seat of our pants. In all seriousness, this is not meant to scare you. This is why motherhood matters. We are looking to the future, their future, and guiding them through every decision with eternity in view. We were serious when we told them we want the best for them, but the reality is that the best is not necessarily their way—*or* our way.

It is revolutionary to mother through the lens of the why as we face our life and family matters, our moments, and even our mistakes.

Teamwork multiplies the motherhood tidal wave of impact.

It would be easier for the builder and me to send a few robots out into the world. Children who do the "right thing" in this culture and follow the trends in education or spending. Teens who date like everyone else and toddlers who have a mind of their own and cannot see the heart of another person. Children raised in a culture of conformity, who leave their homes and begin searching for what matters. But we aren't going to do this the easy way. We will invest in parenting our kids as individuals and with the foundation of God's truths because we will have little to no input about where they will land when they leave us. So with this knowledge, we definitely want to find a partner in someone who knows where my kids are going and where they will land. And this can only be found in Christ.

What Is Your Goal?

If you want to be on the same page as a family, you will need to be reading the same book. The Book. Give your children the why of their future and give them the gospel, and the powerful Holy Spirit will be doing a work unseen to your eyes. Now that's teamwork!

Truth to Live By

Anyone who belongs to Christ has become a new person.
The old life is gone; a new life has begun!
(2 Corinthians 5:17 NLT)

Recognizing the culture of your home and establishing solid, biblical reasons for your structure and way of living will help everyone build a truth-based foundation. Many families establish reasons for how they live and parent based on the pursuit of recognition, desires, or achievement. And others establish a foundation that is a full-fledged pendulum swing in the opposite direction of whatever they experienced in childhood. Our culture is full of generations that have flipped their family dynamics upside down to either create individuals of independence or the extreme opposite, to create those who avoid the world and exposure to its flaws.

When we direct our attention to our mission as moms and understand the vision God has for the family, our purpose will be balanced and focused on the individual, not conformity to our own delicately laid-out pattern. It's a struggle to pull back the curtain of our own thinking and see our family culture for what it truly is. Often I find myself handing out reasons and rules covered with caution tape to my children. My fear or desire for convenience can end up attached to my reasons. Personal add-ons like anxiety, insecurity, or doubt can easily bind children and keep them from reaching their fullest potential in a situation. Do you find that your instructions and rules stem from your fears and doubts rather than from the needs of the situation and a trust in the Lord?

Motherhood is not an experiment where we cross our fingers and hope for a good outcome. We are given gifts to be grown and molded as part of God's amazing plan. The simplest yet most profound job in motherhood is to know the plan and guide children in the plan. Can we do this? Realizing that each child is not a one-size-fits-all creation makes our job complicated; yet it also makes it the most beautiful, interesting job on the planet. We are raising our children for God, and He tells us that motherhood matters.

Taking the Steps

I am excited to see us run this race together in the years to come. I see your children growing right up and alongside my own. I see you learning their strengths and building up their weaknesses. I am championing you as you learn your parenting ruts and ridiculous rules (believe me, we all have them), and as you grow champions who love and live differently than others. We are a team, and so is your family. Here are two next steps to take to build your family team and to honor the individuals who make up that team.

1. We can begin by getting to know our children. I am not referring to being able to list those things that annoy us or the areas in which we think they could do better or aren't living up to our expectations. To truly know them, we will need to engage in conversations with them, spending time together, asking questions, serving them, giving them God, and tending to their hearts. Watch how your child responds, what they lean toward. Let's remember that the way our children bend is not to be swayed by our preferences, but by God's principles.

2. We will need to identify our purpose in all that we do. Most generally, mothers expect obedience and reaction to follow the words, "because I told you so." But if our children's responses to our instruction are to be respectful and timely, it is our job to remember that our expectations should meet a higher standard and not have selfish, unrealistic gain attached. We are accountable to God with our words and rules. Let's raise children who are sensitive to His Word and be careful to avoid conformity.

My Parenting Principle

Children are a gift to be valued and treasured. I want my children to know I am for them and we are learning together. When I feel as if my emotions are overpowering my open mind and the truth that will set my children free, I will set my desires and opinions aside to love them with grace and mercy. It is my job to grow their strengths and weaknesses and to encourage them to be the people God created them to be. I will not get in the way of this, but I will humbly and honestly guide them. His way is my motherhood way, and I will seek out their hearts with all diligence.

Lord, this is one of the toughest areas for me. I realize how easy it is for me to parent with my own purpose and convenience in mind. Will You help me filter my motherhood through the lens of Your plan for my child's life? I need You, Lord. I ask for wisdom in my parenting, my rules, and our family culture to bring everything back to You. Will You walk with me as I prepare to mold the child You have given to me in the time we have together? You are the Creator of all life, and I ask for Your purpose to flow out of the lives in my home. You are my Sustainer. In Jesus' name, amen.

{WHY}
It's Okay to Say No
to Your Children

Any coach will tell you that positive reinforcement is a game changer. But, I daresay, if you stood on the sidelines of a successful team during practice, the players would be hearing an earful of instruction and quite a bit of correction. When we're afraid of using the word *no* in our homes, or we think that guidelines, correction, or rules are going to turn our children away from us forever, then we haven't been paying attention to the example of the most prominent leader in all of history. Jesus led thousands, and His Word continues to lead us in the way today.

This is a given: When I have trouble receiving correction or instruction, I will continue in my folly. In the first few years of my motherhood, I got away with providing a lot more positive reinforcement than correction. I avoided the work of training and correcting. But the time involved and the toll this took on my heart as a mama was too much. When I realized how much more work I had created for myself by avoiding the tough stuff, this truth hit me like a tidal wave and I experienced a parenting crash course. I learned that saying no to a child is not only okay, but it is godly parenting.

Don't Be Afraid to Be the Parent

Many mothers have somehow lost their standing in the home; their children treat them with familiarity or indifference rather than with the full respect, love, and honor a child should have for a mother.

Mothers, we fear losing our children. We birth the long-held dream of this child and we nurse them, care for them, and love them with every ounce of sacrificial love we can muster. And then we realize that life can spiral out of control when lived without boundaries or instruction. It's a hard blow to realize life cannot stay as it is and our children need more discipline, but we fear we will lose their love, their hugs, their presence if we make changes. We have become bullied into parenting under their umbrella of comfort.

Do not parent your children to receive their love. Children thrive with boundaries and structure. Your motivation should be for them and not for yourself. When you realize that surrendering to a child's wants and needs above all else and in every moment is actually *not* in their best interest, you become free to embrace motherhood as God designed it.

Do not parent your children to receive their love...Your motivation should be for them and not for yourself.

God gave us our children to instruct in wisdom and righteousness. How can we do that when they do not love, respect, or even acknowledge the umbrella of protection God gave to them through their parents? Mothers often think they are shielding their children from hardship, discomfort, or stress by letting things go or giving in. The sad reality is that we pull away the umbrella of God-given authority when we let them grow up according to their folly.

When Your Children Are Out of Control

If you were to tell me your children are out of control, I would tell you that you are probably right. If you feel this way, then you have likely lost some control or have never established it. I wouldn't be judging you, but rather trusting your reaction. They are your children, and you are the one feeling the strain of their behavior. As mothers, we get so caught up in our sustaining duties that we forget the foundation that our children need: the teaching and training they require to mature in wisdom and with understanding of consequences. Don't get me wrong. I'm sure your children are saints! But all of us are born with a sinful nature and need wisdom and correction. This is our jobs, mama!

The number one parenting principle overlooked daily in most homes is this: Parenting in the conflict is never effective. It is the daily, moment-by-moment training before the moment of conflict arises that has an eternal impact.

If you think your children are out of control, then most likely, the daily work of instilling character and heart change in their lives is missing. Don't beat yourself up! It's not too late to gain some control. All you need right now is a good start out of the gate and some momentum. Remember, our goal is not to control our children, but to give them the tools to make good decisions—so they can control themselves. When mothers try to control and modify their children's behavior, there will always be pushback.

Truth to Live By

My son, if you accept my words
and store up my commands within you,
turning your ear to wisdom
and applying your heart to understanding—
indeed, if you call out for insight
and cry aloud for understanding,
and if you look for it as for silver
and search for it as for hidden treasure,
then you will understand the fear of the LORD
and find the knowledge of God.
For the LORD gives wisdom;
from his mouth come knowledge and understanding.
(Proverbs 2:1-6 NIV)

With God's grace we can parent with a firm *no* and receive respect and love in return. We often think that a boundary will turn our children away, yet, when they are taught the why behind structure, their hearts and their character will be more sensitive to God's shaping. They will respect and love your godly parenting when it's time for them to make decisions outside of your presence. The why becomes even more important when you aren't there to walk them through life's situations.

What Is the Problem?

Sometimes we tell our children no before we've heard their questions. There will be moments when we cannot handle another request or answer another question, and we use this simple, two-letter word as a reply. You will notice that moments like these have great potential to grow into conflicts. It is important to consider our reply and to discern when we are holding up a definitive no just because we want to avoid inconvenience, confrontation, explanation, or even conversation. Attempt to be aware of the words and actions your child is using to communicate with you. Often, just when I think I know one of my children's motivations for something and I respond with a no, he or she will reply with, "You aren't really listening to me. Did you even hear me?" And sometimes the child is right. I have misread his or her intentions instead of clearly listening to the child's heart and words.

Truth to Live By

Blessed are those who find wisdom,
those who gain understanding,
for she is more profitable than silver
and yields better returns than gold.
She is more precious than rubies;
nothing you desire can compare with her.
(Proverbs 3:13-15 NIV)

Our responses should be weighed with facts and feelings, not our sole opinions or demands. Let's lean on the side of grace. Our responses can be given with a brief explanation rather than the two-letter word that can turn their ears off before we give our reason. Sometimes you do not owe your child a reason and obedience is required in the moment, but discretion is important. Wisdom will balance our responses, and our why will be respected.

Taking the Steps

1. Answer these questions to determine if you are parenting for temporary peace or for lasting impact:

   - Do I feel uncomfortable giving my children boundaries or consequences to their actions?
   - Would I recognize disrespect in my children?
   - Do I wait until I feel the pushing points before I choose to handle a problem?
   - Am I more longsuffering, and do I tend to ignore a problem until it escalates out of hand?
   - What tangible daily practices am I implementing at home to help train my children away from poor choices and behavior?

2. Host a family meeting or begin with small steps like weekly, topical conversations or a posted list of ways to respect each other and God's Word. Create more structure, authority, respect, obedience, and grace-based reactions in your family.

3. Allow God's Word to direct you. Memorize Scripture with your children and on your own as a mom. The truth of the Scripture is always more powerful and convicting than an authority that may not make sense or reach the heart of your children.

4. Remember, it is never too late to model God's authority, love, and grace as a parent.

My Parenting Principle

I am the parent, which means I am never to abuse my authority or allow my children to bully me because I'm afraid of losing their love. If I can lead my children into a way of respect and honor when they are young, their hearts will naturally lean toward listening and discerning why I would ask or tell them to do something. Giving my child a trust relationship will bring them under authority, seasoned with grace. I am modeling God's love to my children even when I am creating and enforcing boundaries. A balance of listening and teaching will be my best friend in motherhood.

Dear Lord, You have led me in trust and obedience. I have learned that You give grace and mercy, and You are still my loving Father. May I model authority with love and grace. Help me teach my children that obedience can be joyful. I delight in You and Your Word. I trust You to guide me in the waters of fear as I train my children in respect, honor, and the purpose of boundaries. Help me not to fear the loss of their love. I know they will become frustrated when they do not get their way, because I do the same thing to You. I pray, Lord, that You will help me to be a good steward of authority. Help my child to receive with a tender heart. In Jesus' name, amen.

24

{WHY}
Can't Means Won't, So Do the Hard Things

My builder is a quiet observer in our home. In all of life he is like this.

We do life together in almost every way, and I have learned one important life lesson from this man: Quiet has a commanding truth to it.

The builder possesses a calm and a gentle nature that our family has grown to respect and pay attention to. I sometimes force my teaching spirit and my verbal love language to hush and remain still, allowing this guy to have the living room floor and the time to win over the hearts of those who watch him and learn. This truth is for all of us. Watching a godly leader is just as important as receiving their words.

When God gave the builder and me this brood, we never, ever expected to have ten so very different children. You better believe when we can have 15-plus people under one roof every Sunday afternoon, our heads and our hearts are turning faster than spinning plates as we try to honor all the personalities and the life-giving love that keeps this unit strong.

Every few years, fear will rear its head in the raising of this crew. Quite honestly, I wake up some days feeling the weight of the job God has given to me and I want to crawl back under the blankets and wave a white flag. Raising bold, brave, and confident children does not happen by mistake or from beneath the covers.

When the first introverted child began to grow lanky and we realized that his quiet demeanor did not match his potentially grand stature, we were a little giddy that we might finally have a "quieter one in the house." We quickly realized he would not speak to others freely and was very content to let his older siblings do the hard stuff, like talking.

The builder would have none of it. I remember thinking that it would be much easier to let this child be the shy, introverted one and let it all roll away. But the builder saw the problem before I could let our son's comfort be his downfall. His quiet introspection was a beautiful thing as he grew up, but his fear and his shying away from being uncomfortable could potentially be a problem. It is important to differentiate the distinction between quiet and fearful. Quiet does not mean afraid, and fear is not from God.

In the evenings, when the family gathers and breaks bread, the builder sits at the head of the long, cherry table crafted with care by the Amish up north, and he watches the family sit and talk with much gusto and love. He will eat his meal and enjoy the rest after a long day of hard work. When he is finished with his last bite, he will push his chair back slightly and rest his arms on the sides of the wooden chair, made just for this time, when he will gather the words he will share with his family. The conversations swing wide from chores, to school, to music lessons, squabbles, and victories. The lanky third-born boy, who was born so fast into this noisy world I was sure he was going to be the overachiever, slowly slinks back into his knotty-cherry seat, hoping the conversation will not land in his lap.

"So your mother tells me you wouldn't pay for the milk at the store counter today and that you can't sing with the family in church on Sunday?"

All eyes are resting on the boy with the bent head and ruddy cheeks. He is not shy. Not one bit. I know, as his mama, what this boy is truly capable of. It's more than he believes of himself, and it is keeping him from living fully.

The builder waits. We all wait for an answer.

"I can't."

"Because you cannot sing? Because you cannot talk to the cashier and hand them the money? What is it, son?"

"I just...can't."

Sometimes one lesson for one person becomes a lifelong saying in a home. This was the night the builder wrote these words onto the hearts of every one of us.

"Can't means won't."

The boy looked up and stared at his dad, waiting for more. Waiting for something else, but that was it. He was given a choice to do the hard stuff.

There are no valid excuses for avoiding something new, stepping out of our comfort zones, or being brave.

Truth to Live By

"Have I not commanded you? Be strong and courageous. Do not be afraid; do not be discouraged, for the LORD your God will be with you wherever you go."
(Joshua 1:9 NIV)

Can't means won't, so never stop trying. This is a message for our children and for ourselves.

Noticing Strengths and Weaknesses

Your innate ability to know your child as only you could will be a strength in your motherhood. You have spent their lifetime studying their gifts and their weaknesses. The hardest part for some mothers (or parents) is to focus on a child's strengths while not ignoring the weaknesses. When we ignore those areas, we are growing a child who cannot face their own weakness. They won't be able to stretch themselves beyond a comfort zone for improvement or for the service of others. We all would be more comfortable doing only those things at which we excel, those things that bring us joy and acclaim or don't cause us discomfort or annoyance. But then we would be a selfish people, thriving in areas that may be keeping us from our fullest potential.

The path of least resistance could allow our children to drift into adulthood rather than require them to take risks and face possible failure or rejection. For our children's strengths to have room to grow, we must identify their weaknesses and those of our home.

Their weaknesses are not those things that annoy us. They're not the things we have learned to ignore or excuse as something they're just not good at. They're not the things that make them uncomfortable. What we settle for is exactly what we will foster in the atmosphere in our home—and in our communication, our standards, our conversation, and our integrity.

For our children's strengths to have room to grow, we must identify their weaknesses and those of our home.

Transforming Their Weaknesses

Transformation begins when our children are tiny and continues into their adult years. Our balance in addressing these areas will take wisdom, humility, timing, and prayer. When our brooding son heard his father speak those words, "Can't means won't," I thought he would push his tall-back chair along the floor and excuse himself in frustration. What happened next is forever etched on my mind. With his long arms folded in front of his chest and his green eyes fixed on his dad, he sat quiet and still. There is a light that turns on in your child's eyes when they have decided to be for or against you or their circumstance. This boy was hard to read; he was always thinking, pondering, and mulling over ideas. But in this moment, his green eyes lit up with shock and truth. He nodded his head, as if we could hear his thoughts, and he excused himself from the table with an odd grin and solemn walk to his room.

That lanky boy now towers over my builder and me. He is a confident leader. He prays big, brave prayers and leads worship for hundreds of people. He is in management in a national business and speaks life into the next generation of children. Because *he can*.

We cannot ignore our children's weaknesses. To do so can be stifling to them and the world around them. The builder and I received a lot of judgement and opinions over this area of our parenting. Many considered talk about weaknesses to be too tough or uncomfortable for our children. But their weaknesses became the very things they would bless others with in the future. When others saw us teaching our children to consider others before themselves, they frowned upon us making them uncomfortable or putting them on the spot. Often our weaknesses will require us to be less "me centered," and more others centered before we can face the fact that our weaknesses affect more than just us. Our children's weaknesses are to be handled with love and grace. There is a balance between building them up and not pointing out weaknesses with a harshness that will stifle their growth. Their weaknesses are the very things that will make them strong.

Truth to Live By

He said to me, "'My grace is sufficient for you, for my power is made perfect in weakness." Therefore I will boast all the more gladly about my weaknesses, so that Christ's power may rest on me.

(2 Corinthians 12:9 NIV)

Motherhood may require you to call out your children, and others may judge you. Motherhood will require you to stand strong in knowing that children who don't do what they don't want to do will face a lot of hard growth when they are adults. Remember why God gave you to your children. Their weaknesses can become their strongest weapons against doubt, fear, and anxiety, but only if they are brought to light and gently and confidently worked on. Be fearless for your children. Do not fear what others think of you. This will be a weakness you may have to overcome yourself.

Draw Out Their Strengths

There is a fine line between raising a child who is full of themselves and a child who knows who they are in Christ. It is important for us to explain to our kids that God gave them their gifts and they are to be used for His glory and purpose.

It's very easy to see and nurture the amazing things our children are capable of and then leave the other areas to just fall into place. Your child will need you to be their champion and their balancer all at the same time.

Can you do this? Is it possible? Yes, but it is going to take practice and prayer. I am sure you don't want to raise a successful gymnast who is unfriendly, ungrateful, or so painfully shy she cannot perform. We don't want to raise highly intelligent computer geniuses who cannot look another person in the eye when speaking or know how to serve others away from the screen.

Encouraging Their Growth

My brown-eyed, grown-up, quality-time girl has the natural ability and desire to include others. With a heart for hospitality and uniting people, she pays attention to details and can rally everyone together to pull off a gathering or event without a hitch. When she was an early teen, she asked permission to host a girls' movie night in our home. With so many sisters, the invitation list was pulled together rather quickly. Her cleaning, recipe plan, and preparing were her strengths. She enjoyed hospitality; it is a true gift of hers. A few hours before the party, I asked her if we could have a little talk. I knew in my gut this was going to be hard. I gently pointed out a few things to her. I asked her if she realized how stressed and tense she had become with her siblings over the timetable and details as she carried out her focused party planning. I knew exactly where she got this from, and this was why it took a spirit of humility to broach this subject with her. Her sisters had basically handed the party over to her because no one was having a good time with the process. Her striving for excellence in all things had led to a painful presence of perfectionism, and it was causing division during what should have been a wonderful time planning together!

I asked her what she might be doing at the movie night in addition to watching the movie. I reminded her that her friends could watch a movie at home, and one of the purposes of bringing the girls together was for fellowship. She shared that girls her age have trouble talking candidly with one another and so the movie was her way to break the ice. I agreed this was a perfect plan, and I offered some suggestions as to how to include everyone, to lead to conversations, and to encourage anyone who might feel awkward. This was the hard part. She had recognized her drive for perfection was an issue, but now she was aware that her hospitality and planning would require her to be aware and considerate of what each girl might require to join in the fellowship with ease.

She took a few hours to process the things we talked about, and then the gathering began. It was beautiful. She and her sisters had pooled their money together to buy ingredients and make the food. They set up the house with fun pillows and a big screen and added games to the evening's options. When I walked through the kitchen, I could hear everyone laughing. Our girl had taken her time to write up a few of her own games and was including everyone, as they all agreed to pause the movie and watch it on their own time. Some of the girls were tucked quietly on the couches and watched expectantly, but she brought laughter out of everyone. When the evening ended, her smile was the biggest blessing. She hugged me and we had a good chat about the value of doing the hard stuff and remembering that God requires every part of us when serving, not just our natural tendencies.

Taking the Steps

Give your children the tools to do the hard things for God:

1. Identify their identity in Christ and their gifts from God.

2. Awaken their hearts and minds to their potential.

3. Find outlets for them to put their gifts to good use.

4. Pray Scripture and God's truth over them.

5. Teach your children what sacrifice is, for hard things do not come easily.

6. Train your children to be diligent and consistent.

7. Give your children the gift of communication. Teach them how to use their words wisely.

8. Always come back to the why of their strengths.

9. Cheer on excellence and not perfection.

10. Pray for humility: Character training will be the biggest factor in helping your children thrive in their strengths.

11. Require practice over laziness.

12. Model balance and perseverance.

13. Encourage them to serve with their strengths.

14. Teach your children to seek and praise the Giver and not the gifts.

15. Don't be afraid to believe God has a big plan for your child.

16. Pray with your children over their weaknesses and their strengths.

17. Remind them that can't means won't.

My Parenting Principle

I cannot and do not want to raise perfect children. If I can bring out the excellence God created them with, He will perform His great work in them. Allowing my children to make excuses when something is hard or only do those things that may be easy is allowing only half of their God-given potential to grow. I can tend their hearts like gardens, pulling weeds and watering their souls. I can foster humility in their lives for change and encourage them to lead with a purpose. If my children's only purpose is to please me or themselves, then I have lost sight of God's complete plan to use their whole lives and not just a part of them. Motherhood is not about raising perfect children in the sight of man, or settling for comfortable when we can be more. I want my children to know more of God and less of themselves; then their weaknesses will be in His strength.

Father God, I want my children to know more of You and less of what they don't want to do or feel they can't do. I pray

earnestly for their strength to be found in You and not in the fear of man or the esteem they have set their minds upon. Help me to show them Your great power in change and grace in growth. Help me to avoid perfectionism, but to seek Your face in the moments I struggle to encourage and foster the fullest potential You have for my child. In Jesus' name, amen.

25

{WHY}
We Hope to Answer
Their Tough Questions

"Mom, can you tell me why any woman would purposefully choose to not have a baby, when babies are a blessing and we believe He is in control?"

I'll be honest with you. Naked-truth honest. This question was handled with gentle care and an answer that went something like this, "All women choose what is best for them. It is your life and your choices before God that matter." Other influences and ideas will come into our children's lives, and they may not be rooted in the same morals or truths you have for your home. We should be careful to prepare our children with wisdom and discernment to meet the ideas and opinions that will come their way.

I am not recommending we isolate our children. We should not create a cultish mind-set. Our homes should not be grounded in judgement or dictating mandates. But, dear mama, your goal is to face their questions before they leave your door. Who knows what your child will encounter when they leave your influence or instruction?

Face the Facts Before They Do

One key component to my motherhood has been learning what my children may face before they actually do. We will not foresee everything, but preemptive parenting always beats out protective and problem-solving parenting. In other words, we have the most amazing opportunity to plan ahead. We will not be able to predict it all, but we want to answer their hard questions and not delegate or hope that someone else will.

Truth to Live By

He decreed statutes for Jacob
and established the law in Israel,
which he commanded our ancestors
to teach their children,
so the next generation would know them,
even the children yet to be born,
and they in turn would tell their children.
Then they would put their trust in God
and would not forget his deeds
but would keep his commands.
(Psalm 78:5-7 NIV)

I have met mothers who are frantic and crazy about what might be coming in their motherhood. They know the topics will be tough, and they are unsure about how to meet their kids where they are. So they lay awake at night worried that they might be missing something. If motherhood were predictable, then long ago someone would've written the only motherhood book we would ever need. But the honest approach for any of us who are worried about providing the right answers to the hard questions is to be sure of what we know and to be honest about what we don't.

Do Not Be Afraid

If you're afraid to talk to your child about the hard things, the scary things, and the very real to life things, then ask yourself this, "If I don't talk to my children, then who will?" You can be 100 percent sure that someone will talk to your children about the questions they have in life, and if it isn't you, the risk can be great. Are you more comfortable if someone more educated or wise in a certain area addresses particular questions? Then seek out godly teachers or leaders and go with your child to meet with them. Be there when they ask the questions; do it together and learn together. Who knows, you may have to do this again. But, mama, do not allow fear of a touchy subject, a scary outcome, or an uncomfortable topic keep you from being real, raw, and open with your kiddos. Your example of honesty, humility, and hope in any situation is the bottom-line life lesson they will walk away with.

While raising seven daughters and three sons, I found myself at the mercy of many questions and discovered this need to figure it out together. I learned quickly that some areas of motherhood will take us by surprise, and some things we can prepare for. I knew with all of our kids that eventually, we would need to address the inevitable. Yes, their bodies were going to change and their desires would follow suit. I was shocked to discover a handful of my friends choosing to avoid these topics and hope for the best. Some things are not best left unsaid.

We chose to create a special weekend about this for our growing young teens. We wanted to create a bonding time of activities, journals, gifts, and simple starter conversations on puberty, sex, and purity. I will never forget my two-day getaway with our three middle daughters. If there were ever three girls more different from one another, it was this trio. Their differences were even more pronounced on a weekend like this, when we were talking about awkward topics and unanswered questions. Our oldest, married daughter offered to join us, which made the weekend even more special and afforded a lot of special laughs and learning for both of us. I love learning with my children; it helps them prepare as mamas to not expect to have it all together or always have all the answers. Engaging in the conversation and bringing our kids back to the truth is a process that will impact their way of seeking information. They will witness and experience good habits that will stick with them. I am challenged daily to raise truth seekers and not opinion followers. We are raising generations today.

The conversations I had with our four girls during that weekend are embedded on my heart and mind forever. After a fun day of shopping, sight-seeing, eating delicious food, and taking in a movie, we finally settled into our hotel room with dessert. We had changed into our pj's and were ready to listen to an audio presentation that covered some of the topics we had already agreed to engage in throughout this weekend. Fueled with chocolate and coffee, with my nerves almost unhinged, I pushed play. What happened next is the perfect example of raising different children and how important our role is as mothers in identifying this and cueing in on their behavior.

As I looked around our hotel room, I felt like I was a behavior specialist. I needed some major counseling in the moment for myself. I wanted to laugh, cry, or lose it with complete hysteria!

To my right, leaning against the back of her bed, one of the girls sat with her arms tightly crossed, eyes closed, and pink earbuds pressed into her ears. She was choosing to not listen to the section about sex. (I don't blame her. I probably would have done the same thing if someone had spoken to me about these things.) She didn't move from that position. To my left sat the wide-eyed youngest of the three teens, with shock registering in her eyes and an almost mortified look on her face. I think she was in shock. She just looked at all of us like we were making this sex stuff up. And straight ahead of me sat my practical girl. I watched as her big, brown eyes stayed focused on the paper in front of her and her pen moved across the page as she furiously took notes. I watched with amazement as she processed facts and her future with seriousness, while the rest of us anxiously awaited the questions we knew she would bring up when the presentation was over.

If humor was not present, I don't think I could have made it through. My oldest, married daughter sat on the edge of the bed listening (she knew the drill, for we had the same weekend, same material, and same outcome when she was younger). Her face kept me present in the moment and more lighthearted in knowing she had survived, and so had I. Now we were in this together.

The audio portion came to a stop. The notetaker looked up from her journal with a smile, the wide-eyed wonder still stared at us with shock, and the girl with the pink earbuds hopped off the bed, walked to the bathroom, and closed the door emphatically behind her. She thought she was done. So began round two of chocolate and water and a fresh, deep breath in preparation for the hard questions and the conversation.

I am challenged
daily to raise
truth seekers
and not
opinion followers.
We are
*raising
generations
today.*

Not every topic was addressed with a serious note. We did our best to keep the mood appropriate for the subject. When we embarked on personal hygiene and personal products, my oldest daughter, in her typical comical spirit, whipped a tampon out of her purse and offered to pass it around and give a very modest description on how to use one. A mix of mortification, laughter, and embarrassment broke up the tension, and we always have a great laugh about this moment today.

It needed to be done, and we did it. It would have been so much easier to throw a book at them and answer their questions if and when they felt brave enough to ask them. It would have been more comfortable to allow my daughter to stay locked behind the hotel bathroom door and not include her in the conversation. It would have been easier to tell them that I figured this out and they could too. Easier is not better. Motherhood will teach you this, and it will also offer you an amazing relationship based on communication and honesty with your kids. Do the hard things, mama, and do them now, before the opinions your kids hear beat you to the punch.

This Will Not Come Naturally

Easier is not better. Motherhood will teach you this, and it will also offer you an amazing relationship based on communication and honesty with your kids.

Mothers think they need to be mind readers. We are always trying to figure out what our kids might be thinking, wondering, or worrying about. We try to pull and pry and meddle. Sometimes we hit the jackpot of a breakthrough, but more often not. I don't know about you, but I don't want my communication with my kids left up to a lottery.

It is going to take work. I know you are ready to close this book right now! Please don't do it. This is where we fall at the feet of Jesus and reach out for help. Every brave step you took to read about the worth of your work will reap rewards. Keep doing the very thing that may feel unnatural to you right now.

It's okay to approach your son or daughter with concerns or topics that they may think are "off-topic," but every topic is a safe place when you approach it with an open mind, grace, and the future in focus. We may think that scaling Mount Everest would be easier than answering their tough questions or talking about those things that no one talks about. If it feels unnatural, consider how different the generations, the church, and our family units could be if doing the hard stuff was the normal thing to do.

When did we become so considerate of our children's privacy or comfort that we stopped asking questions, giving them the truth without fear, and approaching them with questions that may feel like a wedge, but in the end are really expressions of love in all its glory? This kind of love will never come naturally to us until we realize our bent toward comfort and convenience, and then lean in to the real and the raw of our lives. Sure, it is uncomfortable to discuss our physical anatomy and all its purposes. Asking our kids about drugs, sex, and alcohol is hard. Educating, inquiring, and creating boundaries is hard. But imagine the harder stuff. Living with regret is a whole lot worse than being uncomfortable while saying those things that matter.

It may be uncool or countercultural to be the parents who have open lines of communication with their children, but I would certainly like this label better than that of negligent, cowardly, uninformed, or naive.

How Will We Answer Them?

The real question is not whether you will be intentional in pursuing the conversations that we should have with our children. It is, what will you say?

This is where the rubber meets the road. I cannot count how many times I have read Scripture, prayed, and asked for sound wisdom and advice before speaking to my children. It's like a tug-of-war in my mind and a shifting in my heart. It would be easy to give textbook answers to our children when we don't know what to say or how to say it. But we are not raising textbook kids, right?

I want my answers and my advice to be formed with truth and conviction, and I want confirmation that what I tell them has a why attached to it. Someday your explanation will not be enough, and your answers will need to have roots. Deep roots grow conviction if planted in the Word of God. Our opinions will only be laced with strong emotion. Let's be careful to answer our children with both our tone and our reason in tune with our purpose. We are to be *for them* and not our own agenda.

> ### Truth to Live By
> Blessed is the man
> Who walks not in the counsel of the ungodly,
> Nor stands in the path of sinners,
> Nor sits in the seat of the scornful;
> But his delight *is* in the law of the LORD,
> And in His law he meditates day and night.
> He shall be like a tree
> Planted by the rivers of water,
> That brings forth its fruit in its season,
> Whose leaf also shall not wither;
> And whatever he does shall prosper.
> (Psalm 1:1-3 NKJV)

May I plead with you to consider the delicacy of our job? Talking straight to our kids is not to be confused with a burden or yet another thing to get out of the way before they leave home.

Our approach to the delicate and tough matters may determine our children's reactions to our words. There is no getting around the necessity, but viewing it as our duty seems harsh and obligatory. Imagine if we were so comfortable with our God-given roles as open communicators in their lives that our children were drawn to us first—and with confidence and comfort in knowing our reaction is safe and can be trusted.

Remember, talking and teaching before a situation occurs is more effective than doing it during or after. Preemptive love is proactive, and our children deserve our best. Our hearts beat strong and fast for our children at any given time, and our responses can be overly emotional when a conflict or problem arises. Let me encourage you to begin the daily exercise of separating overreactive emotions from the facts of a situation. It is important to remember this as you begin the road to brave discussions and hard topics.

Our desire is for our children to come to us and to allow us to come to them. With open hearts, open minds, and open conversation, your relationship will expand borders in ways you never knew could be possible in today's culture.

I am so passionate about this topic, and it's not because it comes easily to me or because we have done this right from the beginning. The discovery in the process of being brave and embracing our responsibility and privilege opened my eyes to a whole new level of communication, respect (me for them), and trust in a mother-child relationship, which I never would have known existed if I didn't try. We must try. It wasn't easy and it still isn't always comfortable; but I do the hard things, ask the tough questions, and bring up awkward topics because I love my children enough to give them a head start on a focused future.

Be brave, mama. Let this chapter be the shot in the arm that sets you on a forward-moving path toward words that will revolutionize your parenting. Give God the glory for creating motherhood with such intricate beauty and depth. He can give you the strength to begin and to help you find the words you might be lacking. It is always about Him. Motherhood matters are the most important matters and should not be ignored. This is why God gave you to your children and your children to you!

Taking the Steps

I want to champion you in this area over and over because it will take practice and brave, intentional steps into your children's safe spaces. When they open themselves to your words, your wisdom, and your advice, it will be your job to nurture and grow this relationship uniquely. We can remind one another this is a sacred place of trust, and it will be our job to protect the privacy of our children's questions.

The best way to begin is to identify the areas in which your children will need guidance and boundaries. You will never be able to predict the future, but we all surely know we can begin to plan, pray, and prepare for certain conversations.

Here are a few topics you can expect to meet on your horizon of motherhood:

- Modesty
- Privacy
- Friendships
- Strangers and safety
- Boundaries for exposure to pornography, violence, and crude behavior
- Social media
- Language that is hurtful or ungodly
- Bullying
- Time management and stewardship
- Puberty
- Sex
- Abstinence and purity
- Relationships and dating
- Engagement and marriage
- Future

Of course there are many subtopics under each heading above that would depend on the sex and age of your child, but these are the basics you can prepare for now.

Make it happen. Every day is an opportunity to build a stronger relationship and better communication skills with your child. We do not need to wait for the big talks to get into their world. Use your moments wisely. Choose your words carefully, and don't allow their external circumstances and their emotional responses to affect you personally. I believe this is the biggest roadblock for mothers. If we remove our defensive spirit, we can see and hear our children more clearly. This is my challenge every day. I tell myself to get out of the way so I can see and hear and respond to what my children are truly communicating.

My Parenting Principle

A mother invested in the private spaces of her children's lives will never regret the value of creating an open door. Intentional communication, even when it is hard, has much value and builds a forever trust. I will begin to take brave steps to prepare for the hard discussions and tend my own heart to not allow my emotions to get in the way. It is my desire to live spontaneously and intentionally in communication with my child daily and to be a proactive parent, not just preventative.

Father, I need You now more than ever. I thought early motherhood was hard—and then comes this stage with its hard-to-have, tough-topic talks. I am not prepared to do this, and I don't even know how to begin, but one thing I do know is that You promised to walk me through this journey and never leave me. Help me have a heart fearless and brave enough to say the hard things, to be gentle in my words and approach, and to guide me in my timing. Your wisdom is supreme, and I trust You to help me in humility, even when I don't have a good answer. Thank You, Father, for holding my hand in the moments I may falter, mumble, or feel inadequate to do this job. In Jesus' name, amen

26

{WHY}
Teaching Responsibility Doesn't Have to Be Drudgery

Teaching responsibility is one of the toughest aspects of being a mom. It is a backbreaking, relationship stretching, and emotionally challenging task. Most of our motherhood conflict comes from our own frustration, which may turn to anger, over our children's irresponsibility. We shake our heads and vent about our repeated attempts to point out how their negative behavior affects everyone. Have you ever wondered why some families have such responsible, obedient children, while yours cannot seem to figure out this respect thing? The truth is, the majority of families struggle with this very issue at some point in their journey together. And the good news is that there is an answer.

Mama, it begins with us.

You knew I was going to say this, didn't you? I know, it feels as if everything falls on our shoulders, doesn't it? Just to be clear, most of everything we do as moms begins with us, but we don't need to feel the weight of finishing. We are starters, encouragers, trainers, and facilitators. We are the planters and the growers. But God doesn't want us to do the pruning or the harvesting. Allow your seeds of teaching and love to take root and step back when your children have grown tall or strong enough to stand on their own. You are not responsible to carry the burden of their every decision or pursuit. Don't become weary in doing well.

Responsibility is a significant foundation of character and strength that we get to inspire in our kids. It goes beyond chores or picking up one's socks: It is accountability, time management, honesty, diligence, follow-through, investment, and ownership of our actions. A responsible person doesn't allow others to shoulder their emotional burdens, deadlines, finances, accountability, and work.

Truth to Live By
Diligent hands will rule, but laziness ends in forced labor. (Proverbs 12:24 NIV)

We are to own our lives and teach this to our children. We just need a little nudge now and then to remember the end goal in our everyday purpose, even when we want a day off.

The Day Will Come

If you knew me many years ago, as a younger mom, you would have noticed I would do anything for my kiddos to help them, direct them, pick up the slack, and give them a break. I tried to find a balance and thought I was doing okay with this, until a few years ago when my three oldest children were launching out into adulthood and more responsibility was coming their way. The fix-it, find-it, cure-it, mend-it, and tend-it mother came out in me in ways I never knew existed. But one thing I noticed as I watched other moms go before me, launching their own adult children into a new direction, was the struggle they had to let their children fail, fall, hurt, discover new things, and *live out* the very lessons they taught their children as they had been growing up.

It hit me that I could cut my strings gently and still be available to help my adult children without bearing the weight of their decisions as mine to own. I had been leading them for years toward this stage of independence, but now came the hard work of letting go and trusting.

This trusting and releasing can be difficult because we have to watch their lives unfold from afar. We feel the separation from the comfort and help we would've given to them when they were young and learning the lessons under our daily care. I have discovered in myself that I *am* willing to capture their hearts, minds, and actions with the daily investment of teaching, and then release them to learn and live what they have been taught. The day will come when all mothers need to trust that their investment in their child's upbringing will be enough for the future. This is why motherhood matters. Hoping for a good outcome is just not enough. We need to capture their hearts *and* prepare for the release.

What Is Our Responsibility?

The choice is up to us, but in the middle of our decisions, it's important to remember we will reap what we sow. And our children will reap what we choose to sow into their lives. If we choose to make life easy and comfortable for our kids, then they will expect much, struggle with work ethic, and do as little as possible. If we choose to avoid the conflict of follow-through and adhere to accountability, then we will raise a generation that never completes their work and is offended if approached or questioned about it. If we allow permissiveness and avoid ownership of consequences, we will raise adults who have no moral guidelines or convictions and are careless with their decisions, with little regret over wrongdoings or the impact they have on others.

It is serious business to raise responsible children, and this chapter hits hard at the daily work it will take from us as parents. This is *why* motherhood matters. Our children need a moral compass, structure, ownership, and accountability; we cannot count on their child minds to make wise choices on their own. As independent or intelligent as you are raising them to be, responsibility comes from hard work, accountability, and follow-through.

The day will come when all mothers need to trust that their investment in their child's upbringing will be enough for the future.

Do not give up before you have started. I know these words hit hard. I get it, because I have lived it for more than 25 years now. I wake up to the everyday realization that raising my kids means more than providing them with a happy, fun-filled atmosphere where love, hope and peace reign. Yet if we swing the pendulum too far the other way, we have a demanding environment where the pressure to perform and the expectations to succeed are beyond healthy levels.

The Worth of Work

Ingratitude is rooted in laziness and complacency. It's no surprise that children who do not understand the value of hard work and the principle of reaping and sowing have the hardest time with gratefulness. Children raised in a home where responsibility is low on the scale of importance will naturally not have a regard for hard work and their potential. If we constantly do for our children and give to our children, with no practice of productivity in their lives, we can expect to raise irresponsible adults.

Our responsibilities as moms will begin to overlap with the lives and roles of our children. This is where everything begins to get a little fuzzy and confusing to mamas. Yes, we do everything for our children from the time they are born. We feed them, rock them, bathe them, and dress them, but we don't continue those tasks forever, do we? We slowly teach them independence and celebrate their first steps, their first shower, their first day of school. So why is it so hard for us to delegate jobs around the house, transition our children to a structured bedtime, help them manage their money, expect chores to be done, and expect follow-through before we give them more of our time, gifts, privileges, and more?

Truth to Live By

In everything set them an example by doing what is good. In your teaching show integrity, seriousness and soundness of speech that cannot be condemned, so that those who oppose you may be ashamed because they have nothing bad to say about us. (Titus 2:7-8 NIV)

I've heard this on repeat from many mothers: "Children should have a childhood and not have to use their time doing what we can do for them. We want them to have fun and make friends; we want to allow time for homework, play, sports; they will always need more sleep. They will only be children once." Do you believe this too? Is it possible to find a balance here? All those things are true, but not at the expense of a child becoming a healthy and whole person. Remember, our children are growing up before our very eyes. It is difficult for us as mothers because, while our children are growing and changing, our love always stays the same. Yet our love should never excuse our children from accountability or responsibility.

As with everything we incorporate into the culture of our homes, we must find a balance laced with grace. When we teach our children commitment to a work ethic, responsibility for their time and actions, and accountability to authority and their surroundings, we will reap an adult who has a grateful spirit and who values integrity and hard work.

Responsibility needs to be taught and not caught. I want to encourage you here to not fall into the trap of thinking that your child should receive a free pass from this character trait. The most beautiful picture in motherhood is to watch your children own their lives, their actions, their time, and the value of a dollar. We want to have the pride and pleasure of celebrating this with them!

Engage with your kiddos now. It is *never* too late to begin teaching and training your children in responsibility. When you commit to this way of leading your children into adulthood, your home and their lives will be transformed for the future. Let's not view it as work, but as an investment. We can rob our children of accomplishment when we don't allow them the time to learn responsibility. We want to save our children from having to learn these lessons *after* they leave our home. Imagine how far ahead they will be if you don't save them from this wisdom now.

Let's face it: When we put off this form of instruction, the only one we are saving from hard work is ourself. Remember, it takes more work to teach responsibility than it does to do the work for our children. But, dear mom, you will see the fruit of this labor.

Taking the Steps

Let's keep our minds focused on our goal, or we may feel like stopping short before our kids reach the finish line. Teaching responsibility is like passing a baton after running laps around the same track; and when you have handed it over, be prepared to be amazed. Your child will begin to own his or her life and run with it. Here are some places to begin.

1. **Training:** Identify the character traits you are going to incorporate into your child's every day and begin here. This is going to take a hands-on approach for quite a while. You'll need to give them the tools and the encouragement to do their jobs right and to show character while working on them. You will need to model a task, a job, a lesson, or a role in which they will follow. A one-time example is not going to cut it. It takes repetition and reinforcement. Learning to embrace the training moment is the reward of motherhood; it isn't drudgery. As soon as we learn to live in the moment of teaching and celebrate creativity, our children can embrace another new part of their lives and we move on together.

2. **Consistency:** Teaching in small, creative ways will look different for every person. But consistency is vital because someone else is always affected by our choices. When we train our children to brush their teeth every day, we are considering their health. When we ask them to take care of the pet or clear away their plates after dinner, it might seem mundane, but such requests are teaching them responsibility. Always consider the effect the opposite of our actions would have on the world around us, and we will find a motivation for every aspect of our lives. Give your children the why, so their efforts will be consistent.

3. **Follow-through:** This is for you, mama. Motherhood is always about follow-through. We worry about all the things that would go forgotten, missing, or left undone if we didn't follow through. This doesn't mean we're going to take on everyone's lives, jobs, chores, or homework. We are just going to be intentional about bringing them along for the follow-through. When your family forgets to say thank

you for hospitality shown to them, do you apologize and thank others on their behalf, or bring your children back to a point of gratefulness and verbal acknowledgement? Follow through, mom, but do not own your children's lives for them.

4. **Mean what you say and say what you mean:** Often the hardest thing for mothers to do is to follow through on quick, honest, real-life consequences once they state them. We speak with so much emotion in the midst of conflict, it is a miracle our families can even understand us at times. We declare nonsensical consequences for a lack of responsibility and find it hard to live up to our own declarations. "You are grounded for life. You cannot go out in public for a year. No youth group for a month." Where do we come up with this stuff? It is survival sparked with emotion. But, as the builder sweetly chides me, "Mean what you say and say what you mean." Carefully weigh your words and give precise instructions. Confusion muddles expectations, and a mother's emotions mixed with instruction can be confusing. Stay calm and speak life. We want to light their fire and not put it out.

My Parenting Principle

Every good investment a mother makes requires character and work. These are the two truest forms of responsibility I can teach to my children. It is going to take perseverance and diligence on my part to model this for my children to see.

I will put their future ever before me and hold the hope of all they will become as my motivation when I feel too weak to follow through in my investment of teaching and training. Responsibility does not happen by mistake, and I want to pass the baton to my children as they leave my home so they will be able to journey through their lives with strong character.

God, I am tired just thinking of the many years ahead. Help me, Lord, with my perspective, my pursuits, and my strength. I need Your true rest and confidence as I pick up this baton daily. I desire to be joyful in this, but the responsibility I imagine ahead can overwhelm me. I ask for added grace in this. Will You fill me back up as I seek You? Help me to see the faces before me as blessings to be grown, and help my spirit to be strong. You are my strength and my strong tower. I trust You in this as I lay it at Your feet. Right now, Lord, fill me with Your truth and help my doubt to flee. In Jesus' name, amen.

27

{WHY}
You Don't Need to Count to Three

I bet most of us have used the tactic or approach of counting to three to communicate our seriousness to our kiddos. A lot of us have conveyed the threat of impending discipline when our kids aren't listening, sitting down in the cart at the store, coming when called, heading to bed, staying in bed, picking up their messes, or doing chores—and the one, two, three, three and a half, three and three-quarters, continues. We stretch out their time for listening, responding, and obeying as far as it will go. Initially this feels easier than doling out immediate discipline, but by the end of the delayed countdown, we are fuming, frustrated, and desperate for a new way to end the constant ignoring, lack of obedience, and all-out disrespect for us as mothers. Our feet are tapping the floor, our lips may be pursed, and our fingers are strumming our crossed arms, while we wait ever so impatiently.

Before the Counting Begins

There are many kids being raised right now who obey in their time and on their terms because this is a parenting generation that allows children the freedom to make their choices when they feel like it. But when we adopt this as a parenting philosophy, we are actually hindering a child's potential to respect others or authority in the future. Timely obedience nurtures character and responsibility in our kids both now and in the adult they will become.

First-Time Obedience

You do not have to count down to three ever again. I mean it. This sounds revolutionary and slightly miraculous, doesn't it? It is a life-line of training in obedience and saves hours and days of drawn-out, repeated battles with your children. Some say first-time obedience lacks grace. I say grace and second chances in obedience are God's call.

Truth to Live By

My son, do not despise the LORD's discipline,
and do not resent his rebuke,
because the LORD disciplines those he loves,
as a father the son he delights in.
(Proverbs 3:11-12 NIV)

Giving our children more time to choose obedience allows them more time to not listen. Allowing more time for our children to wait gives them more time to choose if they will obey. First-time obedience conveys love, grace, honor, and respect, all rolled into one. It is simple. No adding time to the end of three. No repetition or wondering if three will be enough. No more clever tricks once three doesn't work. Tricks, bribery, motivational stickers, and timers are not going to work when your child was told to hold your hand and not cross the road until it is time. In real-life scenarios that require first-time obedience, there isn't time to train the child. For example, if your child steps into the street and a car is coming toward them, your prayer will be for them to immediately obey you when you call them to step back or to reach for your extended hand. This is a dramatic scenario, but it is a good example for us to look at. This is a circumstance when a parent would be incredibly thankful that they had trained their child in the practice of first-time obedience.

First-time obedience is characterized by your child looking, listening, and obeying when spoken to. No counting, no bribery, no yelling, or stomping of the feet. There is no need to grab their sleeves, strip away privileges, or ground them in their rooms (with their toys that likely distracted them in the first place). With a firm, spoken request or instruction, obedience is achievable. The weary words and repeated instructions are wasting your time and providing your child with a false sense of grace and a disrespect for authority and honor. Grace is not a tapping of the foot, a deep sigh when our children do not respond, or a voice raised to get their attention.

Second chances are not about patient parental behavior. We confuse our children when we give them the freedom to choose how and when they will listen and react. We are giving them time with a short fuse—an impatient and sometimes ungodly response. This is not grace. It is frustrating and confusing.

First-time obedience is characterized by your child looking, listening, and obeying when spoken to.

Grace-Based Obedience

When you call to your children and they do not answer or reply to your instruction, they are being disrespectful and rude. When you give them more time to reply or ignore you, your waiting turns into annoyance and your annoyance is relayed in your tone, intensity, and frustration. This is not grace. We focus on giving our kids grace in our motherhood, but when our own parenting tactics frustrate us, then we have a problem. We create a dichotomy when we give kids more time to be obedient, while fuming and tapping our feet at their inability to respond to a system we set up for them.

Truth to Live By
Children, obey your parents in everything,
for this pleases the Lord.
(Colossians 3:20 NIV)

Children who know that the expectations placed on them are rooted in love, patience, and understanding are often very obedient; they learn the joy of listening and responding at once. We have taken the guesswork out of our expectations. Our children are not left wondering if this is the time you will be upset while counting to three, or if you will grow weary of the follow-through and lose your patience. They are aware that obedience brings joy and they discover the lack of frustration and conflict in their days. It is a win-win.

Taking the Steps

To ease the transition, let's begin with a few questions to identify where you are in your motherhood journey:

- Has my counting become a crutch to avoid an obedience struggle?

- Will my children struggle with this concept, or will I lack the fortitude to train them consistently in obedience?

- Will I be able to be consistent in training my children in first-time obedience?

- Do I understand and believe in the value of this principle?

- What might keep me from training my children in this area and why?

- Am I thinking about the future and the more grown-up child exhibiting a lack of respect, honor, and timely obedience?

Let's begin this together and be willing to engage in this conversation with other mothers so we can encourage them or lean on them for prayer and help. Ask a mentor mom to come alongside you and give you an extra hand as you carve out time to work on this character quality. Here are a few practical tips to get started; the rest is up to you and consistency.

First-Time Obedience Tips

1. Have a family meeting to explain how you are going to work as a team to make a few changes. Carefully explain

and give examples of what first-time obedience will look like in your home. Role-play and laugh a lot.

2. Start small and do not expect your child to grasp or like this new concept right away. It will take time and consistency, mixed with patience and love, to create a home characterized by first-time obedience.

3. Remember the fruit of the Spirit (Galatians 5:22-23). Encourage your child to be joyful, and remember to put on your own patience and self-control.

4. Follow through with consequences when your child forgets or refuses to listen.

5. Celebrate obedience and continue to praise your child for trying as you continue this process.

If you have older children, it is not too late to introduce the idea of listening with respect and honoring your instructions with a timely response. All of us can use some practice in honor and respect. Obedience is an external action of the heart. Begin today.

You are on the road to revolutionizing the atmosphere in your home and the tender places of your child's heart. Obedience is an external reaction to a well-tended heart grown in respect and honor.

My Parenting Principle

First-time obedience is not a manipulative means to get my way. I believe it is a symptom of the heart, and it is my job as a mother to nurture respect, honor, and joyful obedience in my children. When I focus on externals only, my child will grow in resentment and misunderstanding of obedience and will never embrace the godly motivation for obedience. I will demonstrate the fruit of the Spirit as I work with my children in character growth, so that I may not show hypocrisy in my actions and my heart will grow tender to the learning process and struggles they may have.

Dear Lord, am I able to run this long race of teaching and train-ing without growing weary? Every day there is so much to learn, train, accomplish, and be patient through. I'm afraid I am failing my children, and I am more aware than ever how much I need Your wisdom and Your strength. Today I choose to put on Your whole armor and go to battle over my chil-dren's hearts. Will You help me to not lose sight of the deeper places where the real work is being done and the battles should be fought? Help me to see past their behavior and straight to their hearts. Lord, if I am overlooking their lack of obedience because I am weary, open my eyes so I can walk humbly in the difficult places for my children, rather than choosing to make excuses to skip the hard work. You are my strength and my Redeemer. I will find refuge in You today. In Jesus' name, amen.

28

{WHY}
Your Focus Will Become Their Future

With our firstborn son finally napping in the corner of our one-room, third-floor apartment, I finally found time to sit and cool off from the intense heat we felt every day in the South with no air conditioning and tight living conditions. It seemed like the day was going to go on forever. In fact, every day in this season of my life seemed to rest on uncertainty and afforded me no peace for my future. I was a young mother in a strange land, following my husband to Bible college and still trying to figure out who I was as a woman.

Was this what it was like to be a wife, a mother, and a Christian, or was I missing something? When I look back on those years, I realize I was stumbling through the journey of knowing who I was and what God wanted me to do with my life. Most girls my age were in college or just now celebrating their engagement—and here I was, married, with a son, and living far away from family or friends. It was a time like no other in my life. I learned more about who I was and who I wanted to become. But more importantly, I learned who God wanted me to be.

I fought against accepting God's plan for my future, and my focus settled in on survival. I merely moved through the motions of motherhood and attempted to act courageous in the face of every new day.

I will never forget the moment, as my son quietly napped and I tried to find something new to do in our small space, when the builder walked in the door with an excitement on his face that flooded the room. His words were coming out of his mouth faster than my mind could process. Something about a trip to Africa, a missionary meeting, and the call on his life, our lives, to seek the Lord with all our hearts.

I stopped hearing anything beyond the word *Africa*. The next thing I knew we were sitting in a tiny room full of other students, chairs tightly fitted together, with our son on our lap, considering a life in Africa serving as missionaries. I turned my heart off right there and stopped listening to the world. I remember it distinctly to this day. This is where I began to own my life. Everything came into focus right there in that tiny room, where big decisions were before us and the word *Africa* became a distant memory.

Own Your Life

Our lives changed after this meeting. When the builder told me he thought going to Africa might be good, I asked why. When we evaluated whether to spend more time in school, I asked why. And when we found out we were to have another baby, I asked, why now? All of a sudden, I realized I needed to know why God wanted me to be a mother and a wife, and what this meant for me with the builder and our family. Author Sally Clarkson says, "Owning my life means taking responsibility for my own behavior, decisions, and attitudes, so I may become all God created me to be and leave a legacy that points to Him."[2] I wanted to own my life fully.

Truth to Live By

Love GOD, your God, with your whole heart: love him with all that's in you, love him with all you've got! Write these commandments that I've given you today on your hearts. Get them inside of you and then get them inside your children. Talk about them wherever you are, sitting at home or walking in the street; talk about them from the time you get up in the morning to when you fall into bed at night. Tie them on your hands and foreheads as a reminder; inscribe them on the doorposts of your homes and on your city gates. (Deuteronomy 6:5-9 MSG)

The year we faced the whys was the year the builder and I became a team. We were not forging ahead with our individual goals and aspirations. Our dreams and focus became one. We didn't go to Africa. My builder finished his Bible college degree and we headed home to the north. We had a beautiful baby girl and returned home to discover the bigger calling God had on our lives.

We chose to seek His face and pour our lives into an investment of raising our family, building our business, and stewarding the gifts God gave us uniquely. Marriage is a sacred union to protect and cannot be lived in its fullness until there is a focused unity. We became united as we prayed Matthew 6:33: "Seek first the kingdom of God and His righteousness, and all these things shall be added to you" (NKJV).

It is not that Africa and more years of Bible college were wrong, but we knew that for us, stewarding the small was our first step to being used by God.

Where Is Your Heart?

Small moments are where the hidden gifts are waiting. You will need to focus on discovering why God gave you your gifts, your calling, your future before your children can understand their own foundation.

I was learning to live each day with spiritual intention. I evaluated my choices through a lens focused on how each decision could be used by God. My moments were laced with promise for the future and how my life could point to Jesus. Everything came into focus, and our life was full of possibilities.

God was molding me, pruning me, and stripping away ideals, expectations, and perfectionism, because when I set my focus on Him, He planned to use it.

When we let God have our lives, He gives us a focus for every moment. Our future becomes a story in the making—one that we could not have directed or planned so well if we had tried. I realized that my focus would become my children's future. Though the stripping away of my own selfish desires was painful and growing out of my childish ways was a process, I can see how those very ordinary days have turned into my legacy.

Someone recently told me they thought it was nice I was writing a book, but they wanted to remind me that the day will come when my children leave home—and then what will I have?

I smiled and told them that way back when, God reached in and tugged at my heart. I chose to live my life for Jesus and not for my children. Any legacy left here for them is because He has my heart and gives me my focus. My children are just living in my surrender. Wholly and completely given to God. When my children leave home, God is still my first love.

When we let God have our lives, He gives us a focus for every moment. Our future becomes a story in the making.

Perhaps this seems radical. It is. I desire to make a radical difference in the lives of my children. When I surrendered my plan and my selfish desires and allowed God to guide me in His plan, He gave me a new focus, and it wasn't on myself. It was for the future.

Truth to Live By

Start children off on the way they should go,
and even when they are old they will not turn from it.
(Proverbs 22:6 NIV)

This is the message I hope your heart will resonate with. I love my children with everything in me, I have given everything I know to give them and more. If there were only one thing I could leave them as a legacy, it would be a focus on eternity and the value of living a life fully surrendered to God.

I could never lay out the best plan for each of my children, hoping they make it through the unexpected twists and turns of life. But I know I can trust a sovereign God to direct them, if they follow, to the best future ever.

This is my focus every day. When I lean hard into His grace, I remember this moment by moment. My focus is my children's future. How about you?

Taking the Steps

Have you fully surrendered your plan to the Lord? Those ideas, desires, and callings that seem to pull on you stronger than motherhood or His call on your life? This is the hardest stretching, pruning part of a fully focused life for Jesus. May I gently come alongside you in this, and encourage you that there truly is no better plan for any of our lives than the one God has already prepared? A fully focused life doesn't guarantee comfort and freedom from pain. Surrender does not mean a glorious return in the moment. Surrender is giving back what we've been given. The pull of the world can be stronger than the decision to allow our efforts to be unseen for a time. Motherhood's return has a kingdom value, and the rewards are your children's focus and future.

A few questions for reflection might help you explore where you are in your journey.

- Where do my affections lie? Am I seeking pleasure over principle? Do I know why I make the decisions I do and what the end goal is? What am I working toward? Am I exhausted and storing up earthly treasures with no eternal value?

- Have I ever truly surrendered the gifts God has given to me, to be used in His time and for His glory?

- Was there a time I chose to give my life to God? Today is the perfect time to believe He died for me and His plan is infinitely bigger than my own.

- What are my idols? Has my family replaced God on the altar of my focus and my future?

- What are the influences in my life that may be determining my focus?

- Do my children see my diligence and efforts as part of His plan?

- How can I let go of my own control and let God have my motherhood too?

My friend, if your life seems to be in a tailspin, do not be disheartened. Let this sink deep and resonate with you today: God is on the throne. Motherhood is a daily surrender, and God sees all the hard stuff, even when no one else can. May our focus be on the One who is our strength.

You are not alone in your motherhood. If you feel your life has been robbed of excitement, your dreams, and your plans, perhaps it is time to discover the abundant life God has waiting for you. Walk with me in the truth that He will never leave you or forsake you. Even when your children move out or choose another way, you are never alone.

My Parenting Principle

It is easy to move through life following my emotions and making decisions based on desires. I realize that my focus will become my child's future. I desire to see my motherhood through the lens of Christ and not through my own convenient, carefully laid out plans. My family should not become my idol, and I am willing to focus on His infinite plan for all of us. A focused family with an eternal pursuit will produce kingdom changers for generations to come.

Father God, You are my first love. I know my children will leave my arms someday. I want to rejoice in this moment when it comes and not be grieving over something lost. Your plan is beautiful, and my motherhood is a work in progress, but I know that with my daily surrender to You it can reap an eternal reward. Help me, Lord, to keep my mind on You. When I feel like faltering and taking back control, give me the peace to know that my children are Yours too. I am waiting on You daily to keep my focus when everything in me wants to dictate a future and a plan for all of us. Help me live a surrendered life, so my children will know You are God. In Jesus' name, amen.

Let's Talk

Here we are, at the end of a lot of words and perhaps a whole lot of doubt or conviction. I wish we were sitting together and having this conversation as we finish this book. I would want to tell you personally a few things that the words here may not have been able to relay. I would want you to know the real me, the one a typed page cannot show you. My emotions and my trials, my bumps and bruises as my pride was stepped on while typing these words. Because I am a woman with feelings, that has allowed my fear of man and the trap of comparison to dampen my mood and quite frankly hinder my motherhood on many occasions.

Your heart may feel bruised and battered or a bit torn up right now. Your children may be grown, or you may be waiting to be a new mama any day now. Wherever you are in your season of mothering, may I appeal to you with a whisper of hope? I want to remind you that your legacy will live on, whether you feel like you have gotten it all wrong or you're afraid you will not do everything right. When we give our children a reason to live and to love, when we give them a why, a legacy is born.

Move in a little closer here for a moment: I am going to tell you something in this quiet space that I may not repeat again to anyone else. I fear motherhood every day. I fear myself and my inability, my lack of knowledge, my inexperience in every new season. I fear that my mistakes will define my children forever. I fear losing them, watching them walk away from everything we knew; and I fear failure. But fear is a stronghold; and so, every day, I wake up, shake the fear off, turn my eyes to Jesus, and whisper a prayer for strength and purpose. I ask God to help me give my children a reason to live and a reason to die. And for everything in between, I ask God to help me live in obedience to Him.

When a day is all said and done, I know I have done my best. His best. If I give my fear over to God, He can do immeasurably more than I could have ever asked for.

Here we sit together, and perhaps we have never met. There is always this part of me that feels the need to show you my imperfections and to tell you my struggles, with the hope you will know that I am not any different than you. I fear comparison, because I want others to know the reality of where I have come from and the path I chose to get where I am today. Motherhood is defined by surrender. I chose not to surrender my motherhood to fear, comparison, or to the trap of discouragement or pride.

If you take away only one message from reading through this section together, let it be this: Let God have your motherhood, and He will give you the joy and the reason you have been searching for. It will be contagious and flow over and into every area of training, teaching, and living you do with your children.

What will be the focus we give our children today? Are we truly giving them a reason to change, or just a handful of to-do's that may have a desirable outcome? Let's give them a why and let God determine the rest.

You are so loved and not alone. I wish I could send you off with a warm pumpkin muffin that my daughters now bake better than myself, and give you a hug. I hope you will know the richness of His abundant grace on your life.

Don't be afraid to tell someone your struggles, and let God have the glory in the repairs. He is the ultimate reason why motherhood matters.

{WHY}
Your Motherhood Matters

My womb does not give life anymore. There are mornings I wake with my hand resting on my stomach and remember. I remember every movement over the last decades—the stretching and the growing and the birthing. Those spaces within me are empty now, but my name is still Mother. Every dream birthed my heart did not live in my arms, but the stretching and learning and giving was still part of my journey. While I know my hands and heart are full, I still long to feel that life again. The bond of growing a life and birthing a dream begins with a seed of hope. The hope that our motherhood will mean something and that everything we do might matter.

The womb may be empty, but hope remains alive. Having a mother's heart means that you and I will bear down into the seasons for those we love. My hand rests on the back of my grandson, to comfort or console. My hand smooths down the blonde wisps on top of my granddaughter's head, and my heart rests firm in knowing that motherhood matters and continues into the next generation.

When I see your arms empty, I mourn and pray with you.

When I watch your heart relentlessly pulled in another direction, I cheer for motherhood to capture your eye and fill you with life.

When I know of your deep struggle at home or with your children, I feel the pain. I know it to be real, and I kneel and ask God to give you the forever grace to hold on to this dream, even when the daily effort gets hard.

When I meet you and see your juggling act, I lend you my hand and tell you it is okay to let something go.

And when we gather together, I will champion you in every way possible. I will champion your vision, your story, your differences, and your loss.

You can do this well because God has equipped us all. You are in the right place, where differences complete us and words enlighten us. You are called to make a difference. We are raising generations today!

Your motherhood matters. Because you matter!

Acknowledgments

To those who believed this message from the beginning to the end and ushered me into an obedient yes, I am in debt to you, and you have my gratitude and friendship. You celebrated every milestone with me as a labor of love and stuck to the end with me, for better or worse.

To the builder, who shows me undying love and commitment and championed me every single, painful step of the way. You are my hero and have given me more grace than I deserve. You told me that God gave you one job when we married 27 years ago, and that was to support and lead me into my calling. Thank you for listening to the Father and living in obedience to Him. This book has your imprint over every page. We are a team, and this book is another product of our love and communion.

To Ruth for seeing this vision and giving me time as I waited on God. Your patience and perseverance allowed every word to find its place, and I will never forget your commitment to teaching me the ropes. You inspire me.

To Hope, a faithful friend, amazing listener, encourager, and prayer partner, your tireless editing and teaching have forever changed my life. You are the real deal, my friend, and I am honored to have walked this journey with you.

To my faithful friends, for checking in, sending notes, praying, and holding me up on days I thought I would never see the finish line, your investment in this book carried me to the end.

To my children, who wrote this book for me in the very essence of life and allowed me to learn more about God and more about motherhood, I am blessed beyond words to walk through life with you. Your help in picking up the pieces of life we had to set aside for a time— making meals, homeschooling, driving to lessons—and your love and teamwork gave me affirmation that writing this book was the right thing.

To my own mother, who gave me the tools and the confidence to follow my dreams. You loved me well.

To my Father in heaven, for giving me grace along this road. You are my Rock and my Redeemer. You are my story. You called me to this, and I give it all to You.

About the Author

September McCarthy is the wife to one amazing builder and a home-educating mother to ten beautiful children. She is juggling the stages of motherhood, from adult children to toddlers, and is now a grandma to two more blessings. September writes with a heart of compassion for broken lives and shares hope in her words for women in every season of life. She is the founder and director of the nonprofit ministry Raising Generations Today. She hosts annual conferences and speaks nationally to share the hope she holds onto to daily navigate life's waters. September holds no claim on having it all together, and writes with a voice and heart of humility and learning. You can find her words daily penned on her blog, One September Day, at www.septembermccarthy.com. September lives a rural life with her growing family, chickens, gardening, shelves overflowing with books, and a project always on the horizon. Her family is her number one priority, and her heart is always at home. She believes in new mercies every day and fresh grace on everyone she meets.

www.raisinggenerationstoday.com

Notes

1. Gary Chapman and Ross Campbell, *The 5 Love Languages of Children: The Secret to Loving Children Effectively* (Chicago: Moody, 2012), 113–116. Used with permission.
2. Sally Clarkson, *Own Your Life* (Carol Stream, IL: Tyndale, 2014), XVII.